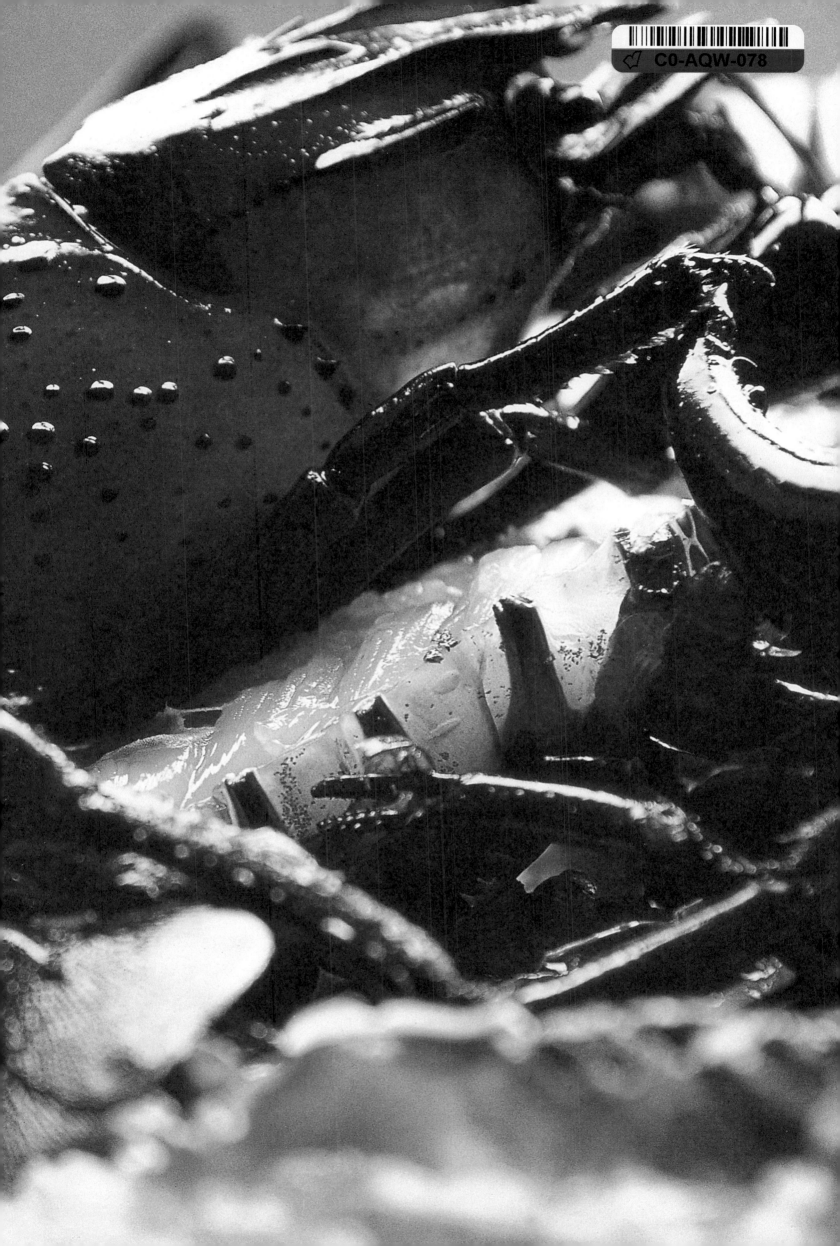

cooking with
boutique winemakers

To Liz Johnson

Best Wishes for Christmas

2002.

From Peter Kimball

& hope someday you can try
the recipe on P109.

cooking with boutique winemakers

Wine-and-food matching secrets
from behind the cellar door

Judith Kennedy

Photographers
Oliver Strewe
and
Ionas Kaltenbach

acknowledgements

Published by:
R&R Publications Marketing Pty Ltd
ACN 27 083 612 579
12 Edward Street, Brunswick, Victoria, 3056
Australia wide toll-free: 1800 063 296

©Richard Carroll

Publisher: Richard Carroll
Author: Judith Kennedy
Project Manager: Judith Kennedy – Boutique Wines Australia Pty Limited
Commentator: Stefano Manfredi
Creative Director: boutiqueartstudio.com
Photographers: Oliver Strewe and Ionas Kaltenbach
Sub-Editors: Greta Thomas and Meg Thomason
Writer/Wine Researcher: Sharon Wild
Researcher: Louise Cole

The publishers would like to acknowledge
and thank the management and staff of the
boutique wineries featured in this book,
for all of their support and assistance,
including the provision of materials for
photography and, especially, their enthusiasm
for making the project a reality.

The National Library of Australia
Cataloguing-in-Publication Data

Kennedy, Judith, 1944 -
Food from the boutique wineries of Australia.

Includes index.
ISBN 1 74022 044 7
EAN 9 781740 220 446

1. Cookery - Australia.
2. Wine and wine making - Australia.
3. Menus. I. Title.

641.50994

First Edition Printed March 2002

Printed in China

contents

foreword

Some time back Judith Kennedy and the Association of Australian Boutique Winemakers dubbed me "the father of Australian boutique wineries". Writing this foreword proves there are parental duties along with such recognition, and what a lusty infant it has proved to be.

Judith Kennedy is an extraordinary woman. She gets things right. We met after both of us had severed connections with the operating theatre. How intriguing is the correspondence of a former surgeon/winemaker introducing a cookbook presided over by a former nursing sister who has become such a leading presence in Australian wine.

Every good winemaker is, or has the potential to be, a good cook. It is just that a winemaker focuses his or her culinary talents on the fruit of the vine. Researching my first book, I had the good fortune to happen upon the late, great winemaker Maurice O'Shea's handwritten recipe book, complete with newspaper cuttings and tip-ins. It was pretty exciting to leaf through it.

Trying out the recipes was almost like sharing those fabulous weekend cook-ups he and his mates enjoyed over the 30s and 40s of the century past. I included some of the easier ones in my early books. Now you have the opportunity to explore much the same pleasures, with these glimpses of the cooking of many of Australia's best small winemakers.

Come, share their table.

Max Lake

introduction

My first experience of the boutique wine community was at a four-hectare vineyard in the Perth Hills in the early 1970s. My brother and his wife, Peter and Helen Fimmel, had planted their first vines and built a small hand-made operation, complete with winery facilities and cellar door.

The most exciting part of our weekend visits was when the closed sign went up on the road and the remaining samples were taken from the cellar door to the kitchen.

"The chardonnay goes best with this and the gewürztraminer goes best with this, and of course the merlot..."expounded the winemaker.

Years later, when I met the people of the wider regional boutique wine industry first-hand, I was further impressed by their love of matching their own wines to favourite foods.

Max and Joy Lake of the famed Lake's Folly, Caj and Genny Amadio of Chain of Ponds, Wendy and Bill Chambers, the Ritchie family of Delatite, Ian Home of Masscni Homes, Louise Cole of Cambewarra, Max Patton of Rothvale, and many more, have welcomed me into their homes, their kitchens and shared their wine-and-food matching secrets. I discovered matchmaking to rival any large city restaurant... and the idea for this book was born.

Our spectacular gourmet trip takes you to Orange with Peter Logan; Allandale in the beautiful Hunter Valley; Canberra, to visit Clonakilla and the Kirk family; the beautiful River Murray with Rockford; the Barossa Valley to Turkey Flat; deep into the southwest to Cullen; Queensland's Sirromet, and the rocky east coast of Tasmania, to visit Apsley Gorge.

There are 80 wine-and-food matching features in this book, each complete with recipe, as supplied by the winemakers.

Come with us on a picturesque journey around Australia, and discover wine-and-food matching secrets from behind the cellar door.

Judith Kennedy

new south wales
and
southern queensland

Most of the subregions throughout this state are represented in the following chapter. One of the smallest and most exciting, subregions is the versatile New South Wales South Coast.

In the past, "sun, sand and surf" described the south coast, with the odd mention of fish and chips!

The pristine beaches of Jervis Bay were the primary attractions, although the hinterland, green and lush, was also worth exploring. Art has also had a notable presence here, with Cambewarra Estate the gateway to Arthur Boyd's gift to the nation – Bundanon.

Regional cuisine has recently undergone many changes, coinciding with the emergence of the young wine industry. Visitors (and locals) have become aware of the diversity of supply – cheese, lush strawberries, orchard-fresh blueberries, honey, delicious fudge and the hot emu pie which has become a ritual for visitors. Local seafood, lamb, beef and poultry are a standout taste experience, and hitting the high notes are the sumptuous oysters from Greenwell Point, the "oyster capital of New South Wales".

Duck eggs farmed here are also gaining in popularity, especially when their richness is used to add a luxurious touch to freshly made pasta.

south coast duck-egg noodles
with mushrooms and green beans

100 g semolina
400 g stoneground, wholemeal organic flour
5 farm duck eggs
3 tsp salt
Sautéed mushrooms and steamed green beans, to serve

Sift semolina and flour, forming a volcano-shaped mound. Break the eggs into the centre and add salt. Incorporate eggs into the flour with your hands, drawing flour mixture into the egg until a coarse paste is formed. If mixture is too sticky, add more flour, using a spatula to scrape the dough together.

Knead dough with your palms on a lightly floured surface. Work the dough for 10-15 minutes, until smooth and elastic. Cover in plastic wrap and rest for 1 hour. Gently roll out dough into a rectangular sheet of pasta 2-3 mm thick, and slice or use a pasta machine to form the noodles. Cook as soon as possible, or dry over a clean coathanger for 10 minutes.

Boil noodles for 5-8 minutes in water with sea salt and a dash of oil added. Strain and top with sautéed mushrooms and steamed green beans. Wonderful as an entrée, or as a side dish with poultry or seafood.

Matches well with oaked chardonnay, rosé, and if you can find a sparkling chambourcin; great match!

Louise Cole
Cambewarra Estate, Shoalhaven, NSW

New South Wales

allandale winery
andrew harris vineyards
bimbadgen estate
blue wren winery
briar ridge vineyard
brindabella hills winery
cambewarra estate
casella wines
charles sturt university winery
clonakilla
cowra estate
frog rock
gartelmann hunter estate
hamiltons bluff
kulkunbulla
logan
macquariedale estate
madew wines
millfield
peacock hill vineyard
rothvale vineyard and winery
ryan family wines
saddler's creek wines
simon gilbert wines
tempus two wines
the silos estate

allandale winery

Hunter Valley

With the stunning Brokenback Ranges at his doorstep, it is not surprising that Allandale winemaker Bill Sneddon is inspired. From seven hectares of vines in the centre of Lovedale, Allandale grows classic Hunter varieties as well as the less widely grown pinots noir and meunier for sparkling wines.

Bill also makes wine with grapes he sources from Mudgee, Hilltops and McLaren Vale. Humble about his winemaking prowess, Bill also quietly goes about whipping up a mighty feast in the kitchen or outdoors at the barbecue.

duck & orange sausages and chardonnay
with rocket, beetroot and onion jam

To make about 7 kg of sausages
5 kg duck meat and fat
2 kg oranges, peeled
500 g pistachio nuts, shelled
100 g salt
30 g ground black pepper
5 g ground nutmeg
1 glass Allandale shiraz
Rocket, freshly cooked
beetroot, and onion jam,
to serve

prepare, cook and serve
Mince duck, oranges and pistachios together, add seasonings and wine and mix well. Stuff into sausage skins, using a sausage-making machine. Refrigerate.

BBQ, preferably over a wood fire, while fresh and enjoy the first glass of chardonnay while cooking. Serve with rocket, freshly cooked beetroot, and onion jam.

Recipe courtesy of AC Butchery, Leichhardt, NSW.

18

Above: Anna, Bill, William and Sally Sneddon.

manfredi's comment
Well worth the modest investment in a sausage-filler, this recipe is a clever take on the classic combination of duck and orange. The hint of citrus acts as a foil for the richness of the duck and its fat, lifting the flavours in the sausage to complement those of the accompanying chardonnay.

andrew harris vineyards

Mudgee

Andrew Harris is undoubtedly a man of the land. His family's background is in agriculture and Andrew maintained his close links to the soil when he and his wife Deb established their own wine business in 1991 in their home town, Mudgee.

Andrew and his team have boundless energy, and this is reflected in their rich, carefully crafted wines. They produce a wide range of styles that please all manner of tastes, both locally and abroad. Andrew thrives on family life and thoroughly enjoys creating wholesome country feasts that he can share with family and friends.

Above: Andrew Harris and his son, Sam

roasted turkey and sparkling shiraz
with macadamia nut stuffing

1 cup long-grain white rice
1/4 cup brown rice
1 cup roasted macadamia nuts, coarsely chopped
6 green shallots, chopped
1/4 cup fresh basil, torn
2 tbsp oil
1/2 onion, finely chopped
2 cloves of garlic, crushed
2 tsp fresh ginger, chopped
1 tbsp grated lemon zest
1 tbsp lemon juice
1 tsp seeded mustard
1/2 tsp vinegar
2 tbsp honey
1 medium turkey
Olive oil, for basting
Roasted vegetables of choice, to serve

make the stuffing
Boil white and brown rice separately and uncovered until tender. Drain and rinse under cold water. Drain well. Combine rices, nuts, shallots and basil in a bowl. Heat oil in a pan and add onion, garlic and ginger. Cook, stirring, until onion is soft. Stir in zest, juice, mustard, vinegar and honey. Bring to boil. Simmer uncovered for about 1 minute, until mixture thickens and darkens. Stir into rice mixture.

roast the turkey
Rinse the turkey under cold water, then pat dry. Spoon stuffing into cavity. Secure wings and legs and place on a rack over a baking dish containing 1 cm water. Brush turkey evenly with oil. Bake in a moderate oven (180°C) for 2-2 1/2 hours until tender. Baste every 20 minutes. Cover turkey legs to prevent burning.

Serve with roasted vegetables of choice. Accompany with a bottle of chilled Andrew Harris sparkling shiraz. Ditto for any cold leftovers!

manfredi's comment
Here's a great way to celebrate a traditional Christmas in Australia – roast turkey and cold sparkling shiraz – a terrific match! The macadamia-and-rice stuffing will help keep the meat moist, and also add lots of flavour.

bimbadgen estate
Hunter Valley

Bimbadgen is the Aboriginal word for lovely views. From the terrace of the estate's imposing Mediterranean-influenced bell tower, the breathtaking views that encompass the Hunter Valley leave no doubt as to the choice of name. The estate's main building houses a state-of-the-art winery, plus a restaurant and tasting rooms.

With a long winemaking tradition in the Hunter Valley, jovial Dutch-born Kees van de Scheur makes a premium selection of wines from Bimbadgen's low-yielding 30-year-old vines (Bimbadgen Estate and Signature ranges), as well as the Grand Ridge selection from the estate's Yenda vineyards. Bimbadgen's Esca restaurant echoes Kees' love of fine food and gives him the opportunity to exercise his culinary skills.

wood-spit roasted duck and shiraz
with shiitake mushrooms, nashi and chilli jam

duck, mushrooms and pear
2 medium ducks
1 head of garlic, 1 bulb of ginger, 2 star anise
50 mL kecap manis and 50 mL water
25 mL sesame oil and 25 mL vegetable oil
200 g shiitake mushrooms
1 large nashi, sliced
1 bunch of choy sum
300 mL duck jus

Prepare wood-fired rotisserie. Remove necks, winglets and cavity fat from ducks. Place half the peeled and sliced garlic, sliced ginger and star anise in cavities. Secure to rotisserie. Baste with mixture of kecap manis and water. Cook for 2 hours, basting regularly. Remove from spit when cooked and dissect into maryland pieces. Keep warm. Heat oils in wok until almost smoking, add mushrooms and sauté. Then add nashi and choy sum, and sauté. Add jus. Simmer. Season if necessary.

chilli jam
700 mL vegetable oil
Large Spanish onion, peeled and chopped
2 red capsicums, de-seeded and chopped
5 birds eye chillies and 3 long red chillies, all de-seeded and chopped
5 cloves of garlic
1 knob of ginger, peeled and sliced
Handful of cherry tomatoes
175 g caster sugar
175 mL fish sauce

Heat oil in heavy pan until smoking. Add onion, capsicum, chillies, garlic and ginger, and brown. Add tomatoes and cook. Add sugar and cook. Fish sauce goes in last. Blend. Cool.

Arrange duck on plates with mushrooms, nashi and choy sum. Pour jus over. Add dollop of chilli jam. Serve with a glass of shiraz!

manfredi's comment
Fashion dictates that duck
and pinot noir are the perfect match,
but I have a feeling that the spiciness
of this dish, together with the chilli
jam, would smother most pinots.
There are quite a few flavours adding
complexity here – the deliciously
charred and caramelised duck flesh,
the sweetness of the chilli jam, and
the spiciness of the star anise and
ginger. What's needed here is a
spicy, concentrated Hunter shiraz
to go head-to-head with such
a grand dish.

23

blue wren winery

Mudgee

James and Diana Anderson purchased the Stoney Creek Road Vineyard in Mudgee in 1998. They worked hard to invigorate their vineyard and nurture their grapes into premium wines, releasing their first vintage under the Blue Wren label a year later.

These wines met with acclaim, prompting the Andersons to purchase a second vineyard in the region, featuring a tasting room, café and restaurant. The Andersons' success is certainly partly attributable to the old, dry-farmed vines that provide them with grapes of an intense, luscious flavour. Their devotion to their vineyards, combined with meticulous workmanship in the winery, ensures they achieve maximum quality from grape to glass.

blue wren plate and semillon
with olive tart and chicken liver pâté

olive tart
1 shortcrust piecrust
2 onions, thinly sliced
Olive oil
8 eggs
600 mL cream
Salt and pepper
150 g black olives, pitted
and cut in half

Blind-bake pie shell. Sauté onions in
a little oil and spread over piecrust. Whisk eggs,
cream, salt and pepper and pour over onions.
Decorate with olives. Bake at 165°C until
egg mixture is set.

chicken liver pâté
1 small onion, sliced
50 g bacon, diced
1 clove of garlic
1 sprig of thyme
250 g butter
400 g chicken livers, trimmed
25 mL brandy
Salt and pepper, to taste

Sweat onion, bacon, garlic and thyme in a little
of the butter in a large pan. Add livers and cook for
5 minutes. Deglaze pan with brandy. Cool mixture
and blend, slowly adding pieces of the remaining
butter, and salt and pepper to taste. Pass through
a fine strainer and set in a mould.

Serve with feta cheese, fried polenta, grilled vegetables
cured meats such as prosciutto or salami, black olives,
salad greens, salsa verde and a bottle of semillon.

manfredi's comment
For casual meals, I think the best
way to eat is the antipasto/meze/
tapas format. This way, there are
lots of little tastes to tantalise
and tease the palate and, for
those of us interested in wine,
it presents a challenge and an
adventure in flavour. Semillon
here shows just how versatile
a wine it is.

briar ridge vineyard

Hunter Valley

The name Karl Stockhausen is synonymous with fine wines of the Hunter Valley, as the man has made many during his illustrious 35 years of winemaking in the region. Karl's boundless passion and enthusiasm are evident in the wines he creates at Briar Ridge, located in the Mount View district of the Hunter region.

The Briar Ridge signature series, comprising semillon and shiraz, is bestowed with the Stockhausen name as a testament to his skills. But Karl's positive energy is not solely directed towards winemaking – the kitchen is another outlet for him to demonstrate his originality and creativity. Seafood is a favourite, as it is an ideal partner for the crisp, tangy Briar Ridge semillon that is a hallmark Hunter Valley style.

lemon-sauced fish and semillon
with risotto and ginger sauce

prepare and serve
Cut fish fillets into bite-size cubes.
Dust fish with flour seasoned with salt and pepper and brush off the excess. Lightly fry in peanut oil or other lightly flavoured oil.

karl's personally designed sauce
1 tbsp each of lemon juice, honey
and finely shredded ginger
1 tsp each of grated lemon rind, fish sauce and mirin
Whites of 3-4 spring onions, finely chopped
1/4 tsp ground black pepper
1 tsp cornflour mixed with 1 tbsp water

Mix all sauce ingredients together, gently heating, and continue to stir until blended.

Karl likes the fish to be served with a mild-flavoured risotto, prepared first as the fish is quick and easy!

to serve
Serve hot risotto with freshly cooked fish, and sauce on the side. Garnish with Italian parsley. Karl chooses his Briar Ridge 2000 Karl Stockhausen Signature Release semillon as a perfect match for this delicious dish.

manfredi's comment
This zesty dish is perfect with a young Hunter semillon. Use a flaky fish such as snapper or red emperor. Classic Hunter semillon's tang is an ideal accompaniment to the sprightly flavours of citrus, fish sauce and mirin in Karl's creation.

brindabella hills winery

Canberra District

Dr Roger Harris left a life of academia behind to concentrate on his passion for wine. By day, Roger and his wife Faye can be found busily tending their vines and monitoring the progress of their wines.

As the setting sun envelops the glorious Brindabella Hills in bright pastel shades, the two like nothing more than to enjoy the panorama as they relax with a barbecue and a bottle of their elegant, spicy shiraz.

bbq smoked lamb and shiraz
with sautéed potatoes and old-fashioned tomato relish

6 medium potatoes
30 g butter
Italian parsley, chopped
6 smoked lamb racks
Steamed zucchini and crusty bread,
to serve

potatoes
Peel, cut, boil, drain well and sauté
in butter until crisp. Sprinkle with parsley.

tomato relish
Place the following in bowl, and leave overnight:
3 kg peeled and diced tomatoes, 1 kg chopped
onions and 1 tbsp salt. Next day boil 1 cup vinegar
with 300 g sugar, 3 tspn each dry mustard
and curry powder, plus pinch cayenne.
Add strained tomato and onion mixture.
Boil gently for 2$\frac{1}{2}$ hours.

lamb racks
BBQ lamb and serve on a bed of tomato
relish with sautéed potatoes, steamed zucchini
and crusty bread. Serve with Brindabella shiraz.

manfredi's comment
Flavours here are those of the smoked and barbecued lamb cutlets and the spicy, tangy, sweet-and-sour of the relish. These predominantly high notes call for an elegant, cool-climate shiraz with structure and grace.

cambewarra estate

Shoalhaven

Louise Cole beams with pride as Simon, her elder son and talented winemaker, lends a hand in the vineyard.
Their picturesque estate and cellar door are located at the foot of the imposing Shoalhaven Mountain.
Louise almost singlehandedly goes about the business of producing award-winning wines from her vineyard,
which features the largest planting of the hybrid variety, chambourcin, on the South Coast.

When Louise isn't in the vineyard or playing tennis, she can be found in the kitchen cooking for family and friends.
Seafood is her favourite, especially when paired with her verdelho or chambourcin.

chilli blue-swimmer crab and chambourcin
with duck-egg noodles

2 large blue-swimmer crabs
2 tsp each of ginger juice,
spring onion juice and white wine
80 g lard
1 tbsp Viva olive oil
2 tbsp brown bean paste
1 cm knob ginger, 1 dried chilli and
4 cloves of garlic, all finely chopped
Light soy sauce
2 tbsp sugar
8 spring onions, sliced into 2 cm pieces
2 fresh chillies, chopped
Duck-egg noodles, to serve
Coriander, to garnish

prepare, cook and serve
Clean crabs and cut into pieces. Crack claws. Marinate in
ginger juice, spring onion juice and wine. Heat lard in a
wok and lightly fry crab until cooked. Set aside. Remove
fat from wok. Add Viva olive oil. Fry brown bean paste,
ginger, dried chilli and garlic until the crackling sound
of the oil starts to die down. Add soy, sugar, spring onion
and fresh chilli. Stir in crab and cook for 2 minutes.
If dry, add water.

Serve with duck-egg noodles and garnish with sprigs of
coriander. Pour a glass or 2 of chambourcin.

manfredi's comment
What a refreshing idea – matching
crab with the ripe, lightly spiced fruit
of chambourcin. These blue-swimmer crabs
have sweet (sugar-soy), sour (ginger juice)
and hot (chilli) flavours that go so well with
the fruit-dominant, unwooded chambourcin.

casella wines

Riverina

Casella Wines is a family-owned business in the middle of the lush Riverina district in Western New South Wales. Its main business is exporting its wide range overseas, leaving only a small portion for sale in Australia.

Filippo Casella was a young man working as a cane cutter in Queensland when he opted for the idea of planting grapes at Yenda. For many years he travelled between two seasonal jobs, cutting cane and tending the vines, in order to provide for his family. Generations later, his sons and grandsons have taken on the hard work in the vineyard, with Joe Casella at the helm. The Italian heritage is firmly in place, with all family members contributing to a lifestyle of good wine matched to traditional foods.

manfredi's comment
Riverina shiraz is perfect with this no-holds-barred traditional Italian lasagne. For a big flavour, use beef; but if you want something a little more subtle try using veal, or a combination of beef and veal.

Above: Phillip and Daniel Casella with their grandmother, Maria Casella

lasagne and shiraz
with tossed salad and crusty bread

6 tbsp olive oil
1 large onion, sliced
2 cloves of garlic, crushed
1 carrot, peeled and sliced
Salt and pepper, to taste
750 g good-quality minced beef
2 x 400 g tins diced tomatoes
375 g tomato paste
Fresh basil, torn
3 tbsp sugar
1¹/₂ L water
Splash of shiraz
3 tbsp cream
Parmesan cheese, grated
Fresh lasagne sheets
1 eggplant, sliced and fried in olive oil
Grated mozzarella cheese as topping
Tossed salad and crusty bread, to serve

cook and serve

Heat oil in a deep saucepan and cook onion, garlic and carrot until soft. Season with salt and pepper. Add mince and brown, stirring to break down lumps. Add tomatoes, tomato paste, basil, sugar, water and wine. Bring to the boil, then reduce heat and simmer sauce for 45 minutes. Add cream and stir. In a large baking dish, layer sauce, parmesan, then a sheet of pasta. Continue the layers, putting a layer of eggplant in the middle. Finish off with layers of sauce and cheese. Sprinkle mozzarella on top. Cover with foil and bake in a moderate oven (180°C) for 20 minutes, then bake uncovered for a further 10 minutes.

Serve with tossed salad, crusty bread and Casella shiraz.

*Above: Phillip, Daniel, Maria, Filippo,
Joe and Kathy Casella*

charles sturt university winery

Wagga Wagga

Charles Sturt University provided Australia's first winemaking degree course in 1975. Since that time, it has not only provided the education for some of our country's finest winemakers, but has become a leading research centre.

The winery, established in 1978, provides a range of styles to suit all tastes, from sparkling, white and red table wines to fortified and sweet ones. These are available from the cellar door, located near the university campus.

Greg Gallagher is proud to be the university's winemaker. In addition to creating popular wines, he loves catching dinner in the local dam.

manfredi's comment
Yabbies are one of the quintessential Australian ingredients and have a delicate flavour and texture all their own. Lime and ginger work very well with their subtle taste. Sparkling wine is the perfect accompaniment for these fine freshwater crayfish.

pan-fried yabbies and sparkling pinot noir/chardonnay
with purple aspen, ginger and lime juice

500 mL sparkling wine
1 L fish stock
20 yabbies
2 tbsp unsalted butter
1 tbsp shredded ginger
12 purple aspens (see note)
6 shallots, finely sliced
Juice and zest of 1 large lime
Salt and freshly ground black pepper
2 extra tbsp unsalted butter, for thickening
Chinese greens and steamed rice, to serve
Straw mushrooms, to garnish

Note: Purple aspen is a scented, high-acid
native Australian fruit. It could be substituted
by fresh grapefruit or lemon wedges.

prepare and serve
Combine wine and half the stock in a saucepan.
Reduce by one third. Remove the underbelly cover
of the yabbies to expose the flesh. In a large saucepan
melt 2 tbsp butter and add ginger, aspen and shallots.
Add yabbies, flesh side down, and sauté for 1 minute.
Add remaining stock, lime juice and zest. Braise
for 2 minutes. Add seasonings and remaining butter
to thicken the sauce.

Serve with Chinese greens and steamed rice, and
garnish with straw mushrooms. Accompany by
chilled sparkling wine.

clonakilla

Canberra District

Tim Kirk returned from Melbourne to join the family business in Canberra in 1996 (his father, John, established the estate in 1971) and set about establishing his career as winemaker. The Kirk family have been instrumental in putting the Canberra District on Australia's fine-wine map with great quality and small quantities of handmade wines.

Tim's love of Rhône-style wines is evident in his elegant, peppery shiraz, to which he adds a splash of the luxurious white variety, viognier, for fragrance. In addition to his love of family and farm life, Tim enjoys the riches of the kitchen and teaching the kids a few of his tricks, though this dish is very much an adult's delight.

crispy duck legs and shiraz/viognier
with fried persimmon and stuffed green queen olives

4 duck legs
1 L duck stock
2 cinnamon quills
2 bay leaves
4 garlic cloves
1 brown onion
2 tbsp brown sugar
2 tbsp lemon juice
3 tbsp vegetable oil
1 L shiraz/viognier
8 green queen olives
180 g goat's curd
1 persimmon

cook and serve
Place duck legs and all ingredients except the last 4 in a braising tray. Mix together, cover and roast for 6 hours at 95-100ºC, adding more stock or water from time to time if mixture begins to dry out. Remove duck and skim fat off braising liquid. Strain. Add shiraz/viognier and reduce until sticky, to make a sauce.

Stuff green queen olives with goat's curd and cut the persimmon into quarters. Set aside. Fry duck until crisp. Add persimmon and olives. Fry until olives shrivel. Serve duck, persimmon and olives on a pool of sauce. A glass of Tim's red is the final essential ingredient!

cowra estate

Cowra

The predominantly chardonnay vines were first planted here a quarter of a century ago. At the lower end of the vineyard is a cosy motel, appropriately situated in Chardonnay Lane.

Company owner John Geber's first claim to fame came when his fruit was used by Brian Croser in several icon wines that put Cowra on the wine map as a source of quality chardonnay grapes. Since then, John and his wife Evelyn's own label has expanded throughout Australia and overseas.

The sweeping vineyards run down to the Lachlan River on the edge of the cosy country town, nourishing not only many vineyards but also an abundance of local fruit and vegetables. Liz and Greg Johnston live on the estate and, while Liz is boss in the kitchen, Greg is the viticulturist and master of the vines! Liz is an experienced and passionate cook and, where possible, uses local produce in her kitchen, including rhubarb from the bottom of her garden.

manfredi's comment
I can picture an early-autumn afternoon on the verandah, the lazy sun going down and a refreshing, chilled rosé served with a still-life of meringues, tangy rhubarb and snow-white mascarpone. This is best served on a large platter so everyone can help themselves.

Above: Liz and Greg Johnston

brown-sugar meringues and rosé
with poached rhubarb and mascarpone

poached rhubarb
1 bunch rhubarb, washed and trimmed
1 cup caster sugar
1 cup Lizard Lane Verjus du Merlot
Zest of 1 lemon

Cut rhubarb into 2-3 cm pieces, combine sugar
and verjus in saucepan and stir over medium heat
until sugar dissolves. Bring to boil, add rhubarb
and cook over low heat until tender but holding
shape. Cool and remove fruit with slotted spoon.
Boil remaining syrup with zest, until thick.

brown-sugar meringues
4 egg whites
1/2 cup brown sugar
1 tbsp cornflour
1 tsp Lizard Lane Verjus du Merlot
250 mL mascarpone, to serve

Beat egg whites until soft peaks form, then, still beating,
add sugar gradually. Fold in sifted cornflour and verjus.
Line a baking tray with baking paper and shape large
spoonfuls of meringue onto paper. Cook in a low oven
(120°C) for 30 minutes and allow to cool in the oven.

Serve meringues with rhubarb, mascarpone and syrup.
Match this dish with a bottle of chilled rosé.

frog rock

Mudgee

An ancient granite boulder resembling a squatting frog provided inspiration for the name of this brand, which leapt onto the wine scene in 1997. Prior to developing their own label, Rick and Jenny Turner grew grapes that were in hot demand by other wineries. Their vineyard is located on the site of explorer William Lawson's original land grant near the town of Mudgee.

Frog Rock wines show pure, pristine fruit in an easy-drinking style. Rick, Jenny and their three children are all involved in the business, utilising their combined expertise in hospitality management, wine marketing and viticulture. In the kitchen, the family's food-and-wine matching skills come to the fore!

grilled pork fillet and chambourcin
with spiced cabbage rolls and truffle mash

marinate the pork
1 kg pork fillet
2 cloves garlic, crushed
6 star anise pods
1 bunch marjoram, chopped
Juice and shaved zest of 1 lemon
1 tsp kecap manis
1 cup chambourcin
1 tsp salt and ground white pepper
2 cinnamon quills
2 tsp ground mace
1 tbsp fresh grated ginger (skin on)

Trim pork of any fat. Combine all other ingredients to make marinade and pour over the pork, coating all sides. Cover and refrigerate overnight.

cook the pork
1 knob butter and 20 mL virgin olive oil
1 bottle chambourcin
1 cup beef stock
Spiced cabbage rolls and
truffled mashed potatoes, to serve

Heat butter and oil in a heavy-based pan. Remove pork from marinade (reserving marinade), dry and sear for about 4 minutes on each side, or until golden brown and firm to touch. Remove and set aside. Make a jus by deglazing pan with wine. Boil on high heat. Add beef stock. Reduce to about two-thirds.

Serve with spiced cabbage rolls, truffled mashed potatoes, the jus and Frog Rock chambourcin.

manfredi's comment
Marinating pork fillet in such a beautiful mixture of spice and citrus will give a nice balance once seared and caramelised. The foxy flavours of the chambourcin should provide an interesting foil to this tangy dish.

gartelmann hunter estate

Hunter Valley

Yorg and Jan Gartelmann's vineyard and busy cellar door are located in the heart of the Lovedale subregion of the Hunter Valley. Since purchasing the property in 1996, the Gartelmanns have set about revamping their 16-hectare vineyard with enthusiasm and passion, to produce classic Hunter Valley styles showing premium-quality fruit characters.

The inclusion of tangy sun-dried tomatoes in this hearty lamb dish hits the high notes on the palate, especially when combined with a Gartelmann shiraz.

mediterranean braised lamb shanks and shiraz
with basil mash

8 french-trimmed lamb shanks
1/2 cup Viva olive oil
2 red onions, finely diced
1 kg button mushrooms
2 cloves of garlic, 3 carrots and 3 sticks celery,
all finely diced
2 rashers bacon, finely chopped
1 cup each pitted Kalamata olives and
sun-dried tomatoes

braising essentials
1/2 bottle shiraz
300 mL beef stock
200 mL balsamic vinegar
200 mL water and 200mL olive oil
Fresh rosemary and thyme, plus sea salt
and black pepper

parmesan cheese discs
230 g parmesan cheese, grated

cook the lamb
Sear shanks in hot oil until brown. Remove from
heat and add vegetables. Sauté. Add shanks, bacon,
olives, sun-dried tomatoes and braising essentials.
Cover and bake for 2 hours at 180°C. Remove shanks
and vegetables. Reduce liquid.

basil mash
Make 2 cups of mashed potato and add finely
chopped basil leaves, while hot.

parmesan discs
Shape parmesan into 12 discs on an oiled tray.
Grill until light brown. Let cool.

Arrange shanks with vegetables, basil mash and
parmesan discs. Garnish with fresh basil herbs.
Serve with generous glasses of shiraz.

Manfredi's comment
When cooking with wine, it's always best to use part
of the bottle you're going to drink with the dish.
There's a symmetry about that that keeps the cook
and the cooking honest. To complement the lively
Mediterranean flavours, the lamb calls for an
elegant, though focused, shiraz.

Above: Gartelmann Hunter Estate cellar door

hamiltons bluff

Canowindra

Established in 1995 by architect John Andrews and his youngest son James, Hamiltons Bluff has grown to over 50 hectares of premium grapes producing two wine ranges and now exporting to the USA. The Canowindra Grossi range of wines supports and promotes an amazing local fish-fossil discovery and is the family's most successful wine, after being selected for the prestigious Qantas First Class International wine list. The Hamiltons Bluff premium range includes the family's first sangiovese – a traditional Tuscan varietal widely regarded as a superb food wine.

The Andrews family, who also own and operate Mandagery Creek Venison in nearby Eugowra, have supplied Michael Manners' award-winning Selkirks Restaurant in Orange with both wine and venison for a number of years.

When the family invite Michael around for a meal, they keep it simple. "What on earth do you cook for an award-winning chef?" exclaims John's wife, Ro. "The key is high-quality fresh local ingredients – Michael usually ends up in charge at the barbecue anyway!"

Right: Michael Manners, John and Ro Andrews, and James and Julia Andrews with their son, Angus

venison and sangiovese
with creamy polenta and green salad

Hamiltons Bluff 2000 Sangiovese was selected to accompany this simple and elegant lunch of venison, creamy polenta with green salad straight from the vegetable garden. Michael seared the thick venison steaks on a hot barbecue for only 4 minutes, seasoning with cracked black pepper. The meat was then left to rest for a few minutes before being served.

"The most important thing to remember when cooking venison is that it is an extremely lean meat and should never be cooked more than medium-rare," explains Michael. "A meal like this is ridiculously simple – all you need is quality ingredients, good company and a nice bottle of wine!"

For a polenta recipe, see Dal Zotto Wines, pp144-145.

manfredi's comment
Simple stuff – grill your venison briefly, make sure it's rare and rest it for a good few minutes before serving. Balsamic vinegar and extra virgin olive oil dressing would work wonders here once the meat is sliced and served with the polenta.

kulkunbulla

Hunter Valley

It started with a dream. A dream to make great wine. A never-ending quest for that perfect vintage and a journey that would be one hell of a lot of fun, no matter what the outcome. This is the ethos of Kulkunbulla, summed up eloquently by their tag-line: *Wine with passion.*

Created by a small group of friends and wine-nuts, Kulkunbulla has made quite a splash in its first few years, winning a trophy for Best Chardonnay in the Hunter Valley Wine Awards with its debut wine. Combining old-world notions of terroir with the latest new-world techniques, the wines express varietal purity and finesse that can only be derived from the most fastidious handcrafting.

pumpkin risotto and chardonnay
with fresh goat's cheese

1.5 kg butternut pumpkin
3 tbsp olive oil
4 cloves of garlic, finely chopped
1¹/2 L chicken stock
2¹/2 tbsp unsalted butter
1 onion, finely sliced
4 shallots, diced
1¹/2 cups risotto rice
¹/2 cup oregano leaves
50 g parmesan cheese, grated
Salt and pepper, to taste
200 g fresh goat's cheese,
and black pepper, to serve

prepare and cook
Julienne enough pumpkin to make 1 cup, then dice the remainder. Heat half the oil in a heavy pan. Add garlic, stock and diced pumpkin and bring to the boil. Reduce heat to a low simmer for 20 minutes. Purée pumpkin in the stock and bring back to a simmer. In a separate saucepan, heat remaining oil and half the butter. Add onion and shallots and gently sweat until onion is transparent. Add rice and stir until coated with oil. Reduce heat to low and add 1 cup of the pumpkin stock. Allow rice to cook, stirring and adding stock as you go, until rice is almost cooked (about 15-20 minutes). Stir through julienned pumpkin and continue to cook until the pumpkin is soft. Add extra stock, if required.

To serve, stir in remaining butter, oregano leaves, parmesan and seasonings. Top with goat's cheese and black pepper. Serve with chilled chardonnay.

manfredi's comment
Such a rich and creamy risotto lends itself perfectly to this outstanding Hunter chardonnay. Risotto is a dish you've got to watch constantly and serve immediately after cooking.
I prefer it when it is quite "wet" – that is, when it is almost soup-like. Pumpkin and goat's cheese work well together as a combination of sweet, tangy and creamy with the texture of Italian rice.

Left: Toni and Gavin Lennard with daughter Zoe and Ross McCann

47

logan

Orange

The grape-stained footprint on the Logan label honours the pioneers who once crushed grapes with their bare feet. Winemaker for the recently established Logan family company, Peter Logan, points out that he prefers to keep his boots on, using more advanced winemaking techniques. Besides, the chilly central highlands, where the winery sources most of its parcels of fruit, are not really ideal for running around barefoot!

In contrast to his ultra-modern approach to winemaking, Peter shows off his earthy passion for epicurean delights. His enthusiasm and zest for good living translate into every aspect of his life.

linguine, prawns and chardonnay
with asparagus

500 g fresh linguine
2 tbsp olive oil
2 tbsp butter
2 cloves of garlic, finely chopped
Zest and juice of 1 lemon
1 red chilli, finely chopped
Green prawns, peeled and de-veined
with tails intact (however many you fancy!)
Sea salt and freshly ground pepper, to taste
¼ cup Logan chardonnay
1 bunch asparagus spears, trimmed
4 tomatoes, seeded and chopped
into 1 cm cubes
Handful of dill

cook and serve
Cook linguine in salted boiling water until al dente. Drain well. Heat oil and butter in a large pan over medium heat. Add garlic, zest and chilli. Cook until fragrant. Add prawns and half the lemon juice. Season with salt and pepper. Cook until prawns are opaque. Add wine and asparagus. Cook 1 minute. Add tomatoes and heat through. Add most of the dill.

Toss linguine through the sauce until coated. Serve with a sprinkle of dill and a drizzle of the remaining lemon juice. Don't forget the chardonnay!

manfredi's comment
The "binding" of the linguine
is achieved by combining olive
oil and butter, a great combination
with prawns as well as with ripe
chardonnay. A touch of chilli
and lemon juice adds zing
to the dish.

macquariedale estate

Hunter Valley

Alongside the new plantings on Ross McDonald's vineyard in the Rothbury subdistrict are 30-year-old dry-farmed vines. These yield tiny quantities of super-concentrated chardonnay, semillon and shiraz grapes that encapsulate the rustic charm of Hunter wines.

When he is not tending his vines, usually accompanied by his dog, Zoe, Ross finds time to give his ultra-modern kitchen a workout. The winter feast for four that he has concocted here is perfectly paired with a voluptuous, earthy Macquariedale shiraz.

Above: Ross McDonald and Zoe

lamb fillets and shiraz
with sun-dried tomatoes

1 cup couscous
1 tbsp butter
1 tbsp dried chicken stock
6 green shallots
Salt and pepper, to taste
4 lamb fillets
Virgin olive oil
2 bunches fresh asparagus, trimmed
1 small red capsicum
15 semi-dried tomato halves
4 cloves of garlic, crushed
100 mL balsamic vinegar

prepare and cook

Add couscous to 1¹/₂ cups of water with butter and stock added, and stir. Add half the shallots and season. Leave to stand. Season the lamb with salt and pepper and brown in a little hot oil. Set aside and then slice into thin strips. Slice asparagus into 6 cm lengths, capsicum into 2 cm pieces, and tomatoes into strips.

Add asparagus to an oiled pan while stirring. When brown, add remaining shallots and the garlic. Cook for 1 minute. Remove and set aside. Add vinegar to pan and boil. Add lamb, vegetables and sun-dried tomato except couscous and stir to blend the flavours.

Serve lamb fillets immediately over couscous. Drizzle with hot pan juices. Bon appétit!

manfredi's comment
The Middle-Eastern and Mediterranean elements represented here reflect two of the most important influences in modern Australian cooking. The addition of sweet balsamic vinegar ties the dish together, ready for accompaniment by a concentrated, spicy Hunter shiraz.

madew wines

Lake George, Canberra District

David Madew is both winemaker and vigneron at this beautiful estate winery opposite NSW's famous Lake George. David and his wife Romilly have added a restaurant – grapefoodwine – to their property and also stage the annual Opera by George!, which is a well-known tourist attraction.

David was a theatre director before succumbing to the lure of the grape, establishing his own wine venture in 1994. He projects his love of German and Austrian wines with his steely, crisp cool-climate styles, and includes this statement on his wine labels: *We make wines we like to drink.*

Though grapefoodwine is catered by the Hyatt Hotel Canberra, David and Romilly get a creative say. David's choice of lamb matched to riesling demonstrates an experimental streak which characterises his approach to life. Red meat and white wine? Give it a try!

baked lamb racks and riesling
with mustard mash and broccolini

2 x 4-bone, trimmed lamb racks
3 cloves of bruised garlic
Thyme, rosemary, 1 bay leaf and parsley
Red wine
Olive oil
Salt and pepper, to taste
120 g broccolini
200 g pontiac potatoes
60 g soft butter
60 mL cream, slightly heated
40 g seeded mustard
Extra salt and pepper, to taste
Tomato relish, to serve

marinate, cook and serve
Marinate lamb racks in garlic, herbs, wine and a little olive oil overnight. Heat oil in a heavy pan. Season and seal lamb until golden, then remove. Wrap bones in foil. Bake at 200ºC for 6-7 minutes.

Blanch the broccolini. Boil the potatoes until soft, then mash, adding butter, cream, mustard and extra seasonings.

Serve lamb racks with your desired garnish, mustard mash, broccolini, tomato relish, garnish as desired, and match with slightly chilled riesling.

manfredi's comment
Here's one out of the box
– lamb with riesling! Since
Madew produces deeply
flavoured cool-climate riesling,
the wine has sufficient body
to accompany big flavours
such as this. It is a pleasant
surprise.

millfield

Hunter Valley

Winemaker David Fatches and marketing manager Rose Evans share a glass of wine in the magnificent grounds of Millfield Farm, situated in the beautiful Mount View sub-region. The ultra-modern Millfield winery building makes a charming yet quirky contrast to the other components of a farm rearing highland cattle.

Bellbirds chime as guests enjoy the classic, food-friendly wines that are hallmarks of the Millfield style. To prove this point, David chooses a robust, eclectic dish that incorporates and accompanies Millfield shiraz as perfectly as a mild day in glorious Mount View.

free-range beef and shiraz
with onions and blue-cheese polenta

2 Spanish onions, sliced
20 g butter
1 tbsp olive oil
4 tsp brown sugar
1 tsp balsamic vinegar
1 cup vegetable stock
3 cups water
1 cup polenta
50 g blue cheese
4 beef rib-eye steaks
Extra olive oil for searing
Millfield shiraz
Salt and pepper, to taste
Oven-roasted parsnips, to serve

the onions
Prepare onions the day before for improved flavour. Slowly cook onions in butter and oil for 30 minutes. Do not brown. Add sugar and vinegar. Stir well.

the polenta
To make the polenta, boil stock and water together. Slowly add polenta. Stir until smooth for 10-15 minutes. Add crumbled blue cheese. Set aside.

the beef
Sear steaks in olive oil. Cook to your liking. Remove steaks from pan. Add wine and seasonings, to pan juice. Reduce to make a shiraz jus. Serve with onions, oven-roasted parsnips, polenta and a bottle of shiraz.

Far left and above: David Fatches and Rose Evans

manfredi's comment
Shiraz is needed to accompany fairly gutsy
flavoured dishes such as this. Free-range or
pasture-fed beef gives a crisper, cleaner flavour
than lot-fed or grain-fed beef, which tends to
have an oilier, richer flavour. This beautiful steak,
paired with a blue-cheese-laden polenta and
shiraz sauce, is a winner.

peacock hill vineyard

Hunter Valley

George Tsiros passion for wine is first revealed by the exuberant welcome at his homely cellar door. Both he and his equally vibrant partner, Silvia, enjoy sharing their wines and showing off their vineyard to other enthusiasts.

Wild ducks make up for an absence of actual peacocks on the hill. In fact, the hill where the vines were planted in 1969 was named after John Jenkins Peacock, who settled in the area in 1841. The winemaking at Peacock Hill is both traditional, as George believes in a handmade approach; and experimental – he uses wild yeasts.

George is the cook in the household and relishes the opportunity to use fresh seafood whenever possible. He believes that a glass of wine for the chef is essential in the preparation of evening meals. This is probably the reason George loves to cook so much!

manfredi's comment
A beautifully balanced dish, this combines flavours that are naturally compatible – the richness of butter; the sweetness of leeks; exotic saffron; moist, full-flavoured ocean trout. I can't think of a more appropriate wine than a handcrafted chardonnay.

ocean trout and chardonnay
with leeks, parsley coulis and saffron beurre blanc

3 leeks, white parts only
60 g butter, for braising the leeks
200 mL chardonnay
50 mL white wine vinegar
Saffron threads
90 mL cream
100 g butter, diced and chilled
3 cups Italian parsley sprigs
Sea salt and sugar, for seasoning
4 x 200 g ocean trout fillets (no bones, please)
Virgin olive oil
Salmon roe, to decorate

make the accompaniments
Slice the inside layers of the leeks lengthways
into ribbons. Wash and drain. Melt braising butter
over medium heat. Add leeks. Soften. Add 100mL
of the chardonnay. Cover and bake at 180ºC for
30 minutes. To make the beurre blanc, place vinegar
and remaining chardonnay in second pot with saffron
threads. Reduce to half and add cream. Reduce again.
Whisk in diced butter, adding one piece at a time, while
over heat. Set aside. To make the coulis, boil parsley
in salted water. Drain. Plunge into iced water. Drain.
Purée in processor and then push through sieve.
Keep going... it's worth it. Season with sea salt and
sugar and set aside.

cook the fish
Heat pan. Brush skin of trout with oil. Cook skin side
first. Turn. Remove after 4 minutes.

Take an 8 cm pastry ring and place in centre of each
dinner plate. Spoon in 2 tsp parsley coulis, and press
down. Remove ring. Twirl leeks around a fork and
slide off onto coulis. Serve trout on top of leeks,
spoon saffron beurre blanc around edges of coulis
and decorate with salmon roe. Serve hot, with
chilled chardonnay.

rothvale vineyard and winery

Hunter Valley

During the few years since Max Patton – a retired veterinary surgeon – and his son Luke established Rothvale, numerous trophies and accolades have proven the boys are onto a winning formula.

Max and Luke's recipe for winemaking success begins with super-premium grapes from their gnarly old vines on a former Tyrrell's vineyard in Pokolbin. Their complete control over every aspect of winemaking is essential to their perfectionism, and their light-hearted, gentle attitude is the icing on the cake.

Cottages dotted around the rambling Rothvale property provide private retreats for visitors. But when Max can get away, he goes fishing and enjoys cooking up his catch of the day.

grilled trout fillets and american-oaked chardonnay
with wine-scented parmesan crust

marinate the fish
Marinate trout fillets in Rothvale chardonnay for 20 minutes. Sprinkle with black pepper and finely grated parmesan cheese.

max's basting sauce
Mash some parmesan, black pepper, and 2 tbsp butter into 3 tbsp chardonnay.

cook the fish
Grill fish in baking dish, basting with sauce until crusty and firm. Do not turn.

Serve the fish on a large platter with mashed pumpkin and steamed asparagus, and garnish with parsley. Oh, and that mandatory glass of chardonnay!

manfredi's comment
There are no compromises here, just gutsy flavours and a bold combination of ingredients producing a big, rich dish for a big, rich chardonnay. Cheese and fish are not often combined, but trout can provide a really good vehicle for this creamy basting sauce. Be sure to grill it long enough for a golden crust to form. With such comforting accompaniments, the big flavours of American oak and Hunter chardonnay really shine.

ryan family wines

Broke, Hunter Valley

William Ryan and his brother Matthew are the fifth generation of the Ryan family to be involved in the liquor industry. The family has 27 hectares under vine at Broke Estate and a further five at historic Minimbah House, established in 1855.

Rather than opting to produce the traditional Hunter varietals, the Ryans decided to plant cabernet sauvignon, cabernet franc and chardonnay, due to their admiration for the wines of Bordeaux and Burgundy. This love of French wine is further reflected in their handcrafted approach – they employ traditional techniques such as barrel fermentation for chardonnay, and varietal blending.

When Will and Matt have time, they like nothing more than to experiment in the large family kitchen. During the harsh winter months, slow-roasted lamb raised on the property is a family favourite, especially with Broke Estate cabernet sauvignon.

manfredi's comment
Slow-roasting a leg of lamb is a sure-fire way of coaxing out all of its flavour. As the cabernet sauvignon is soaked up gradually with the port and the balsamic vinegar, the dish develops a nice tang to balance the richness of the meat.

Above: Minimbah House
Right: Matthew and William Ryan

slow-roasted lamb and cabernet sauvignon
with baked egg tomatoes

2.5kg leg of baby lamb
Sea salt
2 tbsp olive oil
1/3 cup Broke Estate cabernet sauvignon
1/3 cup port
1/3 cup balsamic vinegar
1/4 cup beef stock
8 cloves of garlic, crushed
8 medium egg tomatoes, halved

Place lamb in large pot of boiling water and simmer 15 minutes. Remove and dry lamb. Pierce all over with sharp knife and rub salt into cuts. Heat olive oil in baking dish and brown lamb all over. Add wine, port, vinegar, stock and garlic. Cover with foil and cook in preheated very low (120°C) oven.

four hours later...
Remove foil. Add tomatoes. Cook uncovered for 2 hours. Serve lamb to be sliced at the table. Decorate with tomatoes and reduced jus. Serve with vegetables of your choice. Bring the bottle to the table and enjoy with the family.

leftovers
Absolutely great the next day, cold, for lunch.

Above: Matt and Will with their mother, Bliss, right; and Will's wife Fiona and sons Harry and Rafe

saddler's creek wines

Hunter Valley

"Wine with a difference from a winery with a difference" is the Saddler's Creek slogan, which perfectly sums up its diverse range of styles produced from some of Australia's best wine regions. Co-owner and winemaker John Johnstone not only has 25 years of experience in the industry to his credit, but he also breeds thoroughbreds in the Upper Hunter, which explains the horsy themes of his packaging. Equus is one of his key brands.

John strives for excellence in the kitchen (when time permits) by creating dishes that pair superbly with his wines. Red wine with fish... why not!

manfredi's comment
There's plenty of controversy in this dish. Firstly, parmesan with fish will have traditional Italians cursing, though in this case mixing the cheese with the pinenuts and sultanas softens its impact somewhat. Secondly, tossing bok choy in extra virgin olive oil will have some purists running for cover, but I think it works really well. Thirdly, red wine with fish? Try it and make up your own mind.

Right: Saddler's Creek barrel room

baked eki salmon and merlot
with bok choy and sultanas

2 tbsp brown sugar
2 tbsp mirin
300 g white miso
3 salmon fillets
Extra virgin olive oil
1 tbsp pinenuts
200 g bok choy, sliced
1 tbsp sultanas
Salt and pepper, to taste
1 tbsp grated parmesan cheese

marinate, cook and serve
Melt sugar in half of the mirin. Cool and mix with remaining mirin. Paste mirin and half miso onto a tray. Place a piece of cheesecloth over the mixture, then the fish, and cover with a second piece of cloth. Paste remaining miso over the cloth and marinate fish for 2-3 days in the refrigerator. Remove from marinade and bake in a little oil, just long enough to cook the fish, at 220°C.

Brown pinenuts in a little olive oil and set aside. Toss the bok choy in the same oil. Add sultanas, salt and pepper, nuts and grated parmesan. Cook lightly.

Serve fish over or beside the bok choy mixture. Sprinkle with parmesan. Now pour each guest a glass of merlot, and treat them to a taste experience!

simon gilbert wines

Mudgee

Simon Gilbert's family history in the wine industry dates back to 1842. His great-great grandfather, Joseph Gilbert, a pastoralist, established a splendid vineyard and winery at Pewsey Vale in the Barossa Ranges of South Australia. Simon recalls a particular day, at age 11, when he attended a pre-release of Pewsey Vale riesling. This was the day he decided he was going to become a winemaker.

Simon has almost three decades of vintages to his credit, having gained vast experience in premium wine regions across Australia. His interest in Mudgee as his base was sparked while working there in 1986. Being exposed to the intensity and balance of varietal flavours was enough to convince him of Mudgee's tremendous potential.

manfredi's comment
To achieve the best results, try using mangoes that are not too ripe. Texture is important, so firm mangoes are best for the salsa. The sweetness of the mangoes, the tang of the lime and the heat of the chillies should be balanced – none should be dominant.

lime chilli prawns and semillon/sauvignon blanc
with mango salsa

mango salsa
3 mangoes, peeled and cubed
1 Spanish onion, finely chopped
1 handful coriander leaves, roughly chopped
1 red capsicum, finely chopped
Dash of lime juice

prawns
16 large green prawns, peeled and deveined,
leaving heads and tails on
Juice and grated zest of 3 limes
2 small red chillies, seeded and sliced
20 mL sesame oil
2 extra limes, halved

prepare, cook and serve
To make the salsa, mix ingredients together
in a bowl and chill until serving time.

Soak 16 wooden skewers for 10 minutes in water
to prevent burning. Thread each prawn lengthways
onto a skewer. Mix juice, zest, chilli and sesame
oil and marinate prawns for only a few minutes, as
prawns will toughen in lime juice if left too long.

Cook prawns and lime halves on char-grill, turning
prawns once as they turn red. Remove from heat
and serve with grilled limes, mango salsa and a
chilled glass of semillon/sauvignon blanc.

tempus two wines

Hunter Valley

As the deadline approached for Hermitage Road winery to change its name, Lisa McGuigan reacted in the best way she knew how – by going to lunch with her sales manager, Veronica Lourey. Aided by a steady flow of wine and a Latin dictionary, the two managed to fend off the regulatory French authorities by conceiving their new title – Tempus Two, meaning second era.

Effervescent Lisa takes every opportunity to share some of her favourite dishes – and, of course, Tempus Two wines – with friends.

Below: Tempus Two cellar door

lemon & lime tart and botrytis semillon

6 eggs
150 g caster sugar
100 mL lemon juice
Zest of 1 lemon
50 mL lime juice
Zest of 1 lime
200 g unsalted butter
150 g sugar
23-25 cm precooked sweet piecrust

make the tart
Whisk eggs with caster sugar. Bring juices and zests,
butter and sugar to the boil in top of double boiler.
Pour in egg-and-sugar mixture, while whisking.
Cook, whisking continuously until thick. Strain.
Cool mixture, then fill piecrust. Refrigerate.
Dust with icing sugar before serving.

manfredi's comment
Botrytis semillon is surprisingly difficult
to match with desserts. With its bracing acidity,
there are few sweets that are not overpowered.
This lemon-and-lime tart is perfect in its
simplicity and compatibility.

the silos estate

Shoalhaven

Gaynor Sims and Kate Khoury were looking for a country escape when they fell in love with the Silos Estate – a dairy turned wine estate – on the South Coast. The imposing silos are reminders of the property's past, while the vineyards and winery have been revamped since the pair purchased the property in 1995.

Within a mere five years, the estate has produced attention-grabbing wines (especially its flagship merlot), an award-winning restaurant, and charming guest cottages. Kate even manages to run a children's bookshop in recognition of her and Gaynor's former careers in education. So much for an escape!

green-tea pannacotta and late-picked semillon
with poached pears

300 mL fresh cream
150 mL milk
Rind 1/2 lemon
4 Japanese green tea bags
1/2 vanilla bean
2 sheets gelatine

prepare and serve
Combine all ingredients except gelatine in a saucepan. Boil. Let mixture infuse. Scrape seeds off vanilla pod and return to the mixture, discarding pod. Squeeze tea bags into mixture and discard bags. Soak gelatine sheets in water until soft, then squeeze out. Add to mixture. Cool. Refrigerate in ramekins overnight.

Serve with pears poached in Silos Softly shiraz; and, if desired, fresh fruit. Accompany with a glass of late-picked semillon.

manfredi's comment
Delicate desserts such as this unusual green-tea pannacotta can be overpowered by heavily botrytised dessert wines. The fruit in this dish calls for a late-picked wine without the viscosity or oiliness of heavier stickies. Pannacotta should *just* hold together when unmoulded, with a melt-in-the-mouth texture. The green tea flavour is a wonderful complement to the pear, especially if the pear is poached first in shiraz.

south queensland

ballandean estate
inigo
sirromet wines

ballandean estate

Granite Belt

Ballandean Estate, established in 1931, is Queensland's longest established family-owned and operated winery. The Puglisi family are recognised as pioneering the prestigious Granite Belt. As testament to his devotion to Queensland wine, Angelo Puglisi vociferously and enthusiastically promotes not only his own wine, but Queensland wines generally.

Ballandean Estate wines have performed exceptionally well on the wine-show circuit over the years. Not only that, the estate's cellar door is so popular that it seems no visit to Queensland is complete without stopping by for a taste! In addition to the wines, the characteristically amiable Italian hospitality extends to scrumptious treats on offer at the winery café.

cheese plate and shiraz

with mixed salad and crusty bread

Cheese platters are popular in the Barrel Room Café at Ballandean Estate. This platter features 2 Italian cheeses, montasio and pecorino, sourced from the local delicatessen, and a camembert from award-winning local cheesemakers Warwick Cheeses. Which olives are used varies with availability of local produce, and fresh local fruits are included, according to what's in season. The salads are grown in the family garden behind the winery and the bread is home-made in the café kitchen.

"Our cheese platters are a great accompaniment to a bottle of wine and a great way to while away a few hours in the Granite Belt," says Angelo Puglisi.

manfredi's comment

Care should be taken when serving wine with cheese. For example, blue cheeses can be quite problematic with red wines. Try late-picked or botrytis-affected dessert wines instead; or gewürztraminer. Shiraz works very well with mature hard and semi-hard montasio and pecorino; as well as with reggiano.

inigo
Granite Belt

Bernadette Nicoll has taken over from her mother Janis in The Kairouz Kitchen, a French/Arabic restaurant attached to the Inigo winery at Severnlea. Queensland's Granite Belt is an emerging wine-growing region just north of Tenterfield, best known for its cool-climate white wines.

Bernadette is a descendant of the Kairouz family from Becharre in North Lebanon, where the inhabitants speak French and Arabic. Khalil Gibran, author of *The Prophet*, also comes from there. Inigo is the birth name of St Ignatius of Loyola, the founder of the Jesuits.

Above: Bernadette Nicoll and her daughter, Genevieve

megadarra and verdelho
with spicy meatballs

first, make caramelised onions
1/4 cup olive oil
3 large onions, halved and sliced
3 tsp sugar
1 tbsp balsamic vinegar
1/2 cup water

Heat oil in a pan, add onion and sugar, cook and stir for 5 minutes. Add vinegar and half the water, cook and stir for 10 minutes. Add remaining water and cook a further 5 minutes.

then, make the megadarra
1 cup brown lentils
2 1/2 cups water
1/2 cup white long-grain rice
1 tsp ground allspice
1 tsp ground coriander
1 tsp salt
1 tsp freshly ground pepper
Caramelised onions
Spicy meatballs and cucumber-and-yoghurt salad, to serve

Combine lentils and 1 1/2 cups water in a medium pan. Simmer, uncovered, for about 25 minutes, until tender. Add rice, remaining water, spices, salt, pepper and half the caramelised onions. Cook, stirring, until mixture boils. Simmer until rice is tender. Stir in remaining caramelised onions.

Accompany with spicy meatballs made to your favourite recipe, and make sure you add plenty of fresh coriander and garlic to the mixture. Serve with a salad of Lebanese cucumber slices, lemon juice and fresh mint leaves mixed with yoghurt, and accompany with a cool glass of verdelho.

manfredi's comment
What a wonderfully exotic
dish to serve with mouthfilling
verdelho. Served with refreshing
cucumber salad, the meatballs
are as appropriate on a warm
summer's evening as they are
on a cold winter's day.

sirromet wines

Mount Cotton

It's not difficult to see why Terry and Lurleen Morris, the founders of Sirromet Wines, chose idyllic Mount Cotton as the setting for their winery, which is only 30 minutes by road from Brisbane and the Gold Coast. It was the perfect venue to ignite their passion for food, lifestyle and, of course, wine.

The panoramic views of the rolling vineyards and rural vistas to Moreton Bay and Stradbroke Island provide the backdrop to Restaurant Lurleen's, the winery's restaurant. For the complete experience, local cuisine is paired with Sirromet's outstanding wines.

It could be assumed that Queensland has too tropical a climate for quality wine production; however, grapes for Sirromet Wines are sourced from South Burnett and the Granite Belt, both of whose inland location and high altitude temper the climate and are ideally suited for the production of tangy, fragrant white wines.

seared queensland scallops and chardonnay
with risotto nero and black truffle

100 mL squid ink
800 mL fish stock
3 large brown onions, peeled and
finely diced
100 mL extra virgin olive oil
80 g butter
400 g arborio rice
200 mL chardonnay
Extra 50 g butter
25 Queensland scallops, opened
and cleaned
(5 scallops per person)
1 tsp curry powder
100 mL Viva olive oil
Roasted red capsicums cut into
3 cm rounds
5 finely cut slices of black winter truffle
Tomato concassé, zest of 2 lemons,
chopped chives, and drizzle of
Viva olive oil, to serve

prepare and cook
Add squid ink to fish stock and bring to a simmer. In a heavy-based pot, sauté the onions in the olive oil and first amount of butter until soft and translucent. Add rice and lightly fry until it starts to turn pale golden. This is the most important step, as it opens the grain and allows more liquid to be absorbed. Add the chardonnay and stir until absorbed, then add stock mixture slowly in amounts of 80-100 mL at a time, ensuring that it is absorbed between additions. Cook, adding stock mixture until al dente. Stir in extra butter and remove from heat.

Preheat a heavy pan until smoking. Roll scallops in curry powder and coat lightly with Viva olive oil, then sear quickly in pan. Don't overcook the scallops – they should be opaque in the middle.

Arrange risotto with scallops, and garnish with red capsicum, truffle, tomato concassé, lemon zest, chives and a light drizzle of Viva olive oil.

manfredi's comment

This is a grand dish for a rich and stylish chardonnay. Queensland scallops are more commonly referred to as sea scallops and come as little discs with no roe. They have a milder flavour than the scallops found in southern waters, though they are a little firmer in texture.

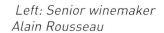

*Left: Senior winemaker
Alain Rousseau*

south australia

Australia's largest wine industry population is concentrated in this state. All of the major subregions are featured in this chapter, and European immigrant families are frequently mentioned as the cornerstones of the business. Let's take a glimpse of the Italian influence in South Australia...

Italian migrants introduced a feast of new flavours and cooking methods into rural Australia, not the least of which were their homemade meat products.

One homeland tradition, which is still widespread, is the killing of the pig and the making of the family smallgoods. This practice involves absolutely no wastage of the carcass and although the condiments and methodology may vary, the fundamentals are the same. It's interesting to note that the further south in Italy one travels, the more pepper and chilli are added to these products, as a better preservative in the warmer climate.

All of these smallgoods are uncooked and salt-cured. The most familiar ones are salsiccia, salami and sopressa (made from minced pork), and capocollo and prosciutto (whole meats). Others include cotecchino (minced rind, from the northern regions); pancetta (bacon), and coppa (brawn, using parts such as tongue and hocks).

Salsiccia, salami and sopressa are sausages of varying sizes, up to 10 cm thick and 40 cm long. The pork meat is minced from fine to very coarse, according to choice.

In Australia, particularly in the cooler southern states, the ritual takes place around mid-year, when there is a chill in the air. Initial curing time for the standard sausage (3 cm thick) is 3-4 weeks; larger sopressa 6-8 weeks; copocollo (neck fillet), 10-12 weeks; prosciutto, from 10-40 days (under salt); then wash them all with red wine and hang to cure for up to 12 months.

the generic italian sausage

800 g lean pork leg or shoulder
200 g fat (to keep the moisture in while curing)
1 tbsp cooking salt
3 g coarse, freshly ground pepper
50 mL red wine
Sausage casing

Mince meat and fat to your choice of fineness.
Mix thoroughly with the cooking salt.
Mix other ingredients in well by hand.
Cover and leave 3-4 hours.

Buy sausage casing from the local butcher (you may have to order it ahead). Run warm water through the casing before feeding onto the nozzle of a sausage maker. Fill until firm. Tie with a loop of white string every 10-15cm. Wash with red wine and hang in a cool place (3-4 weeks). White mould is a good sign. Green mould should be washed off with a mixture of equal parts water and vinegar. Wash with red wine and rehang to cure for up to 12 months.

Serve with fresh, crusty wood-fired bread and red wine, accompanied by giardiniera (pickled capsicum, eggplant and olives) in olive oil and vinegar.

Caj Amadio
Chain of Ponds Winery, Adelaide Hills, SA

South Australia

balnaves of coonawarra
bethany wines
burton premium wines
cape jaffa wines
casa freschi
chain of ponds
fonthill wines
hollick wines
lake breeze wines
langmeil winery
leconfield coonawarra
padthaway estate
peter rumball wines
ralph fowler wines
ravenswood lane
rbj vintners
rockford wines
rusden wines
schild estate wines
simon hackett wines
tapestry wines
turkey flat vineyards
whisson lake

balnaves of coonawarra

Coonawarra

Doug Balnaves became involved in the wine industry in the early 1970s as the Coonawarra manager for a large company. In 1975 Doug and wife Annette planted their own vines on the southern end of the Coonawarra *terra rossa* strip. They sold their grapes to other producers until 1990 – when they decided to produce their own wines. Five years later their winery was built and Pete Bissell, a passionate ambassador of the wines of Coonawarra, joined the team as winemaker.

Balnaves of Coonawarra is a family company, with all members actively involved in the day-to-day running of the business. Doug is general manager, Annette and daughter Kirsty manage sales and marketing; while son Pete is responsible for viticulture and contracting.

Above: Pete, Annette and Kirsty Balnaves

manfredi's comment
This is one of those combinations that is so "out there" it might just work. For best results, use only the finest chocolate. I would suggest staying away from milk chocolate as it's too sweet. Instead use a good dark couverture chocolate with a high cocoa mass (over 60%). This will connect nicely with the Balnaves cabernet.

chocolate ganache tart and cabernet/sauvignon
with blackcurrant coulis and cinnamon ice cream

chocolate ganache tart
250 g flour
2 tbsp cornflour
200 g cold butter, cut into pieces
2 tbsp soda water
Grated zest of 1 orange
2 egg yolks
200 mL cream
300 g quality chocolate
100 mL espresso coffee
Cinnamon ice cream,
to serve

make the tart
Process flours and butter in food processor until the mixture resembles breadcrumbs. Add soda water, zest and egg yolks. Process just until dough-ball forms. Wrap in plastic and refrigerate 30 minutes. Roll out dough and line 18 cm tin. Bake blind until golden, about 20 minutes. Boil cream, then add chocolate. Stir until smooth. Add coffee. Stir. When cool, pour into tart shell. Set.

make the coulis
Combine 250 g blackcurrants, juice of 1 lemon and 1/2 cup caster sugar. Sieve mixture. To serve, spoon some coulis onto an ice-cold plate and then centre a slice of tart on top. Serve with home-made cinnamon ice cream and a glass of cabernet.

bethany wines

Barossa Valley

Bethany was established in 1844 by Silesian migrant Johann Gottlob Schrapel. The winery is now operated by the fifth generation of the Schrapel family, Geoff and Robert.

The Bethany approach to winemaking is based on tradition. The winery, for example, is gravity-fed, as opposed to relying on pumps, as this allows for gentle handling of the wines.

All of Bethany's wines are created from grapes grown on its estate and nearby vineyards. The combination of premium grapes plus careful winemaking results in gorgeous wines brimming with juicy, fresh fruit.

warm prawn salad and riesling
with butter-lime sauce

16 large prawns
Large knob of butter
2 tbsp verjuice
Juice of 1/2 lime
1/2 cup light fish stock
3 shallots, finely chopped
2 tbsp cream
200 g unsalted butter, diced
Witlof leaves and asparagus,
to serve

cook and serve
Sear the prawns in butter. Use verjuice to make a sticky glaze in the pan juices. Toss prawns in glaze and set aside, keeping them warm. To make sauce, place remaining glaze, lime juice, stock and shallots into a small saucepan. Reduce. Add cream and bring back to the boil. Remove from heat. Add 1/4 of the unsalted butter. Stir well on lowest possible heat and continue to add butter, one piece at a time. Once finished, this sauce must not boil, be reheated or allowed to go cold, as it will separate; so make it when you need it and serve immediately!

Serve prawns drizzled with butter-lime sauce. Accompany with asparagus tips, witlof leaves and a glass of riesling.

manfredi's comment
Fruity young Barossa Valley riesling loves seafood, especially prawns. Using verjuice to deglaze the pan picks up the leftover flavours in the bits of prawn that are stuck to the base. This then forms the foundation for the accompanying sauce. As an alternative to verjuice, use some of the riesling.

Above: Geoff Shrapel's daughter, Tania, and wife, Leslie

burton premium wines

Coonawarra

Nigel Burton and Dr Ray Healey simply wanted to produce wines that they could enjoy themselves and share with others. To do so, they set about sourcing great fruit from Australia's premier regions and enlisting top winemaking expertise. The results, not surprisingly, speak for themselves.

Nigel lends his business acumen to marketing the brand. Ray utilises his three decades of experience owning and managing vineyards, as well as his wine-judging skills (he has been chairman of the prestigious Hobart Wine Show), to control production. Their super-premium cabernet sauvignon is a powerful wine showing lovely integration of berry fruit and oak, and reflecting the passion with which it was made.

lamb shanks and cabernet sauvignon
with zucchini flowers and couscous

3 tbsp flour
6 lamb shanks
2 tbsp olive oil
Sea salt and black pepper, to taste
Zest of one lemon
2 birds-eye chillies (no seeds), chopped
2 cloves of garlic, chopped
2 tbsp chopped fresh rosemary
1 cup Burton chardonnay
1 cup veal stock
1/4 cup fresh lemon juice
500 g couscous
1/4 cup chopped Italian parsley
12 zucchini flowers, with zucchini attached

prepare, cook and serve
Flour shanks. Brown in oil. Season with salt and pepper. Push to side in baking dish, add zest and sauté gently until caramelised. Add chilli, garlic and rosemary. Sauté. Add wine, stock and lemon juice to lamb and bake covered for 2 1/2 hours at 180ºC. Remove from oven. Cool. Skim off the fat.

Prepare couscous as directed on packet and add parsley. Moisten 1/2 cup of couscous with lamb cooking juices and stuff into flowers with stamens removed. Steam until just softened. Serve shanks and stuffed zucchini flowers on a bed of couscous, with a glass of Burton cabernet.

Recipe prepared in conjunction with Burton Premium Wines food consultant, Teresa Biet.

manfredi's comment
Flouring the shanks before sealing and braising protects the flesh from fierce heat, as well as providing a thickening agent for the sauce.
Stuffing the zucchini flowers with the couscous is a great idea.
As an alternative, try poaching them gently in some of the lamb's cooking juices.

Opposite: From left, Monique Burton, Teresa Biet and Nigel Burton.

cape jaffa wines

Mount Benson

Cape Jaffa was the first winery to establish a presence in the ruggedly beautiful and relatively isolated coastal region of Mt Benson. The Hooper family owns the estate, with Derek Hooper at the winemaking helm. Cape Jaffa demonstrates that Mount Benson is an area for distinctive, premium-quality wines. Crisp, fresh whites and savoury reds are the specialty of this area, which is also known as the Limestone Coast.

When he's not making attention-grabbing wines, Derek surfs and fishes on the nearby ocean. In pursuing a healthy outdoor lifestyle, Derek is often found stoking the barbecue. He is an easy-going but interested cook, and seafood is often the ingredient of choice.

bbq ocean trout and semillon/sauvignon blanc
with mustard dill cream

2 Cape Jaffa ocean trout
2 cloves of garlic
2 lemons, sliced
4 fresh bay leaves
4 sprigs parsley
4 sprigs fresh thyme
Viva olive oil
Semillon/sauvignon blanc

mustard dill cream
90 g butter
1 cup fish stock
1 1/2 tsp seeded mustard
1 cup cream
2 tbsp lemon juice
3 tbsp chopped, fresh dill
Salt and pepper, to taste

light the bbq, then line up the friends and the wine
Wash and dry the cleaned fish. Place garlic, lemon, and bay leaves into the cavity of the fish. Tie half the parsley and thyme into a bundle and also place in the cavity. Brush with olive oil and place each fish on a large sheet of baking paper and foil. Splash white wine onto fish before sealing the packages. Cook 5-9 minutes each side.

whip up the cream
Melt the butter. Add stock, mustard and cream. Simmer 15 minutes. Stir in lemon juice and dill. Season. Pour over cooked fish. Garnish with the remaining parsley and thyme.

manfredi's comment
Ocean trout is a wonderful fish, rich in oils and extremely versatile and forgiving when cooked. This simple but effective treatment retains all the trout's moisture, ready for the mustard cream sauce to finish. The fresh, grassy flavours of semillon with sauvignon blanc should contrast nicely here.

Far left: Fishing boats in the bay at Cape Jaffa

casa freschi

Langhorne Creek

Casa Freschi is a quality red wine producer, founded in 1998 by David and Tanya Freschi. Their vineyard was planted 30 years earlier by David's parents, Attilio and Rosa Freschi, who immigrated from the Veneto region of northeast Italy, bringing with them their love of the land. David and Tanya share that love and strive to create a beautiful, natural product from the earth.

Today, two ultra-premium wines are produced from the family vines – Profondo (profound) and La Signora (the lady). Both wines express the personality of the land and the passion of the Freschis, who plan their meals around matching great wine to delicious food.

Above: David Freschi, his mother, Rosa and daughter, Isabella Ruby

veal and cabernet sauvignon/shiraz/malbec
with mushrooms

4 tbsp olive oil
l large brown onion, finely chopped
800 g veal, diced
2 bay leaves
Nutmeg
Salt and pepper, to taste
1 glass dry white wine
1 chicken-stock cube
3 whole tomatoes, peeled
1 tbsp tomato paste
1 brown onion, sliced
1/2 cup mushrooms, sliced
Italian parsley, chopped
1 tbsp butter
Mashed potato or polenta,
and salad, to serve

cook and serve
Heat pan, add half the oil and cook chopped onion gently until transparent. Add veal. Seal the meat, then add bay leaves, nutmeg, seasonings and wine. Simmer for 15 minutes. Add stock, tomatoes and tomato paste. Cook until sauce has reduced.

Heat a second pan. Add remaining oil and sauté sliced onion. Add mushrooms and parsley. Mix in butter and simmer.

Serve veal with mushrooms, mashed potato or polenta, salad and a glass of good red.

manfredi's comment
A deliciously classic Italian: Veneto-region veal spezzatino that's big on flavour, with some interesting spice tones with the addition of nutmeg and bay leaf. The accompanying mushrooms are perfect with this quintessentially Australian red made from cabernet, shiraz and malbec.

93

chain of ponds

Adelaide Hills

Giovanni Amadio migrated to South Australia in 1927 from the Marches region in central-eastern Italy and began producing wines soon after. His son Gaetano (Caj), daughter-in-law Genny and grandson Danniel carry on the family business in the Adelaide Hills. Since 1993 they have earned a reputation (and many trophies) for producing premium wines from select parcels of fruit grown in the Adelaide Hills, as well as on idyllic Kangaroo Island.

The Amadio family have a love for world-class wines, fine dining and traditional Italian cuisine – including their own cured meats, which they store in the winery.

Their cellar-door restaurant specialises in elegant antipasti served on the balcony overlooking a vista of gently rolling hills.

roasted kangaroo island marron and riesling

with king george whiting fillets and prawns in beer batter

bake the marron
Cut 300-500 g fresh marron into halves. Lay in shallow roasting dish, flesh up and shell under. Heat 20 g butter, salt and pepper to taste, crushed garlic and 1 tbsp wine in a small pot. Pour half the butter mixture over the marron. Cover and seal. Bake for 10 minutes at 200°C. Increase heat to 300°C. Pour remaining mixture over marron. Bake uncovered for another 10 minutes.

deep-fry the whiting and prawns
Place 200 g flour in a bowl. Make a well. Pour in 1 tbsp olive oil. Add 1 stubby of cold beer as you stir. Whisk until running thin. Refrigerate batter for 1 hour. Dust whiting fillets and shelled prawns in plain flour. Beat 1 egg until thick. Gently fold egg into batter. Don't beat. Batter fish and prawns and deep-fry in a mixture of 1/3 light olive oil, 1/3 peanut oil and 1/3 Suprafry until golden.

Serve seafood on a bed of rice with lemon wedges, side salads and riesling.

Note: Most people over-fry fish, so please be careful not to overcook.

manfredi's comment
This is what I love – three of my favourite seafoods treated with Italian simplicity. Caj's dish is reminiscent of a classic fritto misto, simply served with lemon wedges, fresh salad leaves and maybe some fennel and good extra virgin olive oil. The star is the seafood – uncomplicated by any other flavours – complemented by Caj's delicious riesling.

Left: Caj Amadio in the cellar-door kitchen

fonthill wines

McLaren Vale

The Ansaar family have been growing grapes for 6 years. Recently, the Ansaars have been keeping small parcels of grapes to create their own range. Silk Shiraz shows the distinctive McLaren Vale generosity of ripe fruit complemented by opulent, silky tannins.

Their new vineyards include some unusual grapes, such as the Spanish Rioja varietal, tempranillo. The family is passionate about the potential of such diverse varietals and sees them representing the long-term future for Fonthill.

fillet steak and shiraz

with tasmanian blue cheese and rocket salad

5-6 kipfler potatoes
1 tsp vegetable oil and 40 g butter
4 pieces fillet steak
45 g Tasmanian blue cheese
1/4 cup milk
2 tbsp finely chopped spring onion
Extra blue cheese, for garnish

cook and serve
Boil potatoes until tender. Heat oil and half the butter. Sear steak on both sides. Mash potato with remaining butter, blue cheese, milk and spring onion.

Serve steak with mashed potato and rocket salad, and garnish with a wedge of blue cheese. Serve with shiraz.

rocket salad
Combine lettuce, rocket, snow peas, spring onions, cherry tomatoes and pecan nuts. Dress with combined balsamic vinegar and olive oil, salt and pepper to taste.

manfredi's comment

Sometimes all that's needed to accompany a great bottle of red is an excellent piece of beef, simply seared rare to medium-rare.
The blue cheese in this case adds a tangy balance. Be sure to rest the fillet for five or so minutes, to help the meat relax and "set" its juices before serving.

Left: Ansaad Mohamed, his wife, Jane, and daughter, Laila

97

hollick wines

Coonawarra

When Ian Hollick arrived in Coonawarra in 1972 to manage vineyards for a large wine company, it didn't take him long to recognise the region's potential for producing outstanding table wines. With his wife Wendy, he went on to establish his own vineyard and winery. Hollick Coonawarra Cabernet Sauvignon, released in 1985 – only their second vintage – was awarded Australia's most highly esteemed wine prize, the Jimmy Watson trophy. The rest is history.

"The expression of Coonawarra" is the Hollick catchphrase, and succinctly sums up Ian's carefully crafted wines. They show ripe yet delicate fruit characters and well focused, compact structures; a special feature of the region's *terra rossa* (clay loam) soil. The Hollick sparkling merlot is one of a kind, and Ian recommends its use for medicinal purposes with breakfast, when just a touch of decadence is in order.

manfredi's comment
This very casual dish relies for success on the very best ingredients – good crusty rolls, the freshest spinach, and top-quality smoked salmon such as that produced by Springs in South Australia. Just add hollandaise, and wash it down with Hollick sparkling merlot.

ouefs hollique and sparkling merlot
with hollandaise sauce

hollandaise sauce
4 egg yolks
4 tsp lemon juice
Generous pinch of salt
Pinch of cayenne pepper
200g unsalted butter, melted
Egg yolks, lemon juice and seasonings

Whizz egg yolks, lemon juice and seasonings in the food processor for a few seconds. With the motor running, slowly pour in hot butter.

oeufs hollique
6 free-range eggs
1 tsp white vinegar
50 g baby spinach
3 ciabatta rolls
100 g smoked salmon

Poach the eggs in water, with vinegar added. Steam the spinach until just wilted. Layer the spinach on the ciabatta, then add a slice or two of smoked salmon. Place eggs on the salmon and top with hollandaise sauce. Voila!

Pour yourself and friends a glass of Hollick sparkling merlot and seize the day!

lake breeze wines

Langhorne Creek

The Follett family have grown grapes at Langhorne Creek since 1880. But it was only in 1987 that the fifth and sixth generation decided to take the next step and produce their own wines under the Lake Breeze label.

Their homestead, Bernoota (an Aboriginal word meaning camp among the gum trees), lends its name to the Lake Breeze flagship shiraz/cabernet sauvignon blend. From the precious, stately old vines, Greg Follett carefully crafts the wine, which exemplifies the unique characteristics of this treasured fruit: lip-smacking, chunky berry flavours, grippy yet ripe tannins, and a seemingly endless finish.

fillet steak and shiraz/cabernet sauvignon
with char-grilled capsicum and herbed mash

char-grilled capsicum
Quarter 2 capsicums (one green and one red)
and remove seeds and membranes.
Grill skin side up, until skin blisters
and blackens. Cover for 5 minutes.
Peel skin and slice capsicum into strips.

steak and sauce
Pan-grill fillet steaks to your taste, remove
and keep warm. Add 1 tbsp of oil and
chopped onion to pan juices and cook. Add
balsamic vinegar, home-made tomato sauce,
splash of red wine and soy sauce. Simmer
for 2-3 minutes until slightly thickened.
Pour a glass of wine for the cook!

herbed mash
Make some mashed potatoes, adding crushed
garlic and torn fresh mint.

Arrange char-grilled capsicum on a plate. Mound
the herbed mash and steak on top. Top with sauce.
Sprinkle with chopped parsley, and pour the wine.

manfredi's comment

Here, the sauce made from deglazed pan juices, balsamic vinegar, tomato, red wine and soy brings the whole dish together. Its sweet-tangy character binds nicely with the fine tannins of the Bernoota shiraz/cabernet, creating a lively taste experience.

101

langmeil winery

Barossa Valley

Langmeil was the original name given to the town of Tanunda, established by Prussian settlers in the 1840s. It was around this time that vines were first planted there and the district began to thrive. In the 1980s, the region experienced tough times and the Australian government paid growers to pull out their old vines. The Langmeil vineyards lay in ruin.

Then in 1996, three long-established Barossa families banded together and rejuvenated one of the original vineyards in order to preserve a cherished piece of Barossa history. Now the legendary name of Langmeil lives again, and its wines are luscious and jam-packed with succulent fruit from vines up to 155 years old. They are classically handmade, bold Barossa styles.

Above: Winemaker Paul Lindner

osso buco and old vine grenache
with creamy potato mash and gremolata

4-6 pieces osso buco
1/2 tbsp plain flour
2 small onions
Knob of butter and 1/2 tbsp peanut oil
8 roma tomatoes, pre-roasted
Celery, garlic, turnip and carrots
2 tbsp tomato paste
11/4 cups dry red wine
11/4 cups chicken stock
Bouquet garni
Thinly pared rind of one lemon
Creamy potato mash, green beans,
and crusty bread, to serve

make the osso buco
Coat meat with flour. Brown meat and onions in butter and oil in a large casserole. Remove meat. Add all other vegetables. Cook for 5 minutes. Add next 5 ingredients. Add meat, cover, and bake for 2 hours at 160ºC.

combine the following to make gremolata
2 tsp chopped Italian parsley
Finely chopped zest of 1 lemon
2-3 cloves of garlic, finely chopped

Serve osso buco sprinkled with gremolata. Accompany with creamy potato mash, green beans, crusty bread, and the essential ingredient of Old Vine grenache.

manfredi's comment
I tend to prefer slow-cooked dishes like this osso buco with deep-flavoured, complex wines, such as Langmeil's Old Vine grenache. Slow cooking, especially in wine, brings out the most from the more gelatinous cuts such as brisket, cheeks and in this case, the shanks, producing a classic, lip-smacking dish.

leconfield coonawarra

Coonawarra

Leconfield, situated in the Coonawarra district on the famous *terra rossa* soils, was established by Sydney Hamilton in 1974 and named after an ancestor, Lord Leconfield. It is now owned and managed by Sydney's nephew, Dr Richard Hamilton.

The winemaking philosophy of Leconfield is to produce powerful, fruit-driven wines – a style that is immensely popular with Australian wine-drinkers, and that is perpetuated by the current winemaker, Phillipa Treadwell. The cabernet sauvignon is classic Coonawarra – rich plum and cassis characters complemented by a solid tannin backbone and nuances of new French oak. In other words, a big gutsy red!

wattleseed-infused kangaroo fillet and cabernet sauvignon
with native pepperberry, smoked ham, radicchio and cabernet jus

marinate the kangaroo
Combine 2 tsp ground wattleseed,
2 tsp native pepperberries and 1 cup cabernet
in a saucepan. Heat. Cool and add 1 cup
vegetable oil and 4 kangaroo fillets. Cover
with plastic wrap and refrigerate overnight.

make the accompaniments
Sauté 400 g diced smoked ham and
800 g sliced radicchio in olive oil.

Make a rich jus with browned onions, cabernet,
beef stock, flour, butter and seasoning.

cook and serve
Drain and dry meat. Sear at high heat
and cook to taste. Serve with ham and
radicchio mixture and cabernet jus, with a
glass of Leconfield cabernet alongside.

Above: Cellar-hand Mark Fennel

manfredi's comment
The most important thing to remember here is not to
overcook the kangaroo. It is a lean meat and the fillets
should only be seared for 30-60 seconds on each side,
according to thickness. Once cooked, rest for at least
5 minutes before serving. Rich and intense flavours call
for a well-structured, powerful wine with fine tannins.

padthaway estate

Padthaway

The stately Padthaway Estate homestead (built in 1882) remained a family residence until it was sold to Dale Baker and Ian Gray in 1980 as luxury accommodation. The new owners now concentrate on producing traditional-method sparkling wines and handmade table wines. Winemaker Ulrich Grey-Smith is at the helm.

A historic outbuilding on the property now functions as the Padthaway Estate cellar door. The homestead and gardens make an idyllic retreat, especially when enjoyed with a glass or two of vibrant, sparkling wine and some country cooking.

Above: Ulrich Grey-Smith

marron and sparkling pinot noir/chardonnay
with slow-roasted tomatoes

¼ cup olive oil
8 ripe roma tomatoes, halved lengthwise
Salt and pepper, to taste
8 fresh marron
1 lime, cut into wedges
2 sprigs parsley, chopped
1 tbsp lime juice
1 tbsp vinegar
½ tsp mustard
Rocket salad, sauce,
and lime wedges,
to serve

prepare and serve

Drizzle half of the oil over tomatoes, add salt and pepper, and slow-roast at 100°C for 3-4 hours. Add marron to boiling water with lime wedges and parsley. Simmer for 5 minutes. Cool under cold tap or dip into iced water. Shell and clean. Save heads for garnish.

Make a sauce by mixing remaining oil, lime juice, vinegar and mustard.

Serve cold marron with the slow-roasted tomatoes, rocket salad and lime wedges. Drizzle with sauce and garnish with marron heads.

manfredi's comment
When preparing something as special as marron, it's always best to keep it simple. The marron should be only just cooked, to retain both flavour and texture. Plunge the marron straight into iced water to stop it from overcooking. The roasted tomatoes add body, the dressing adds zing and the Eliza sparkling pinot noir/chardonnay adds luxury to a great dish.

peter rumball wines

Adelaide

Peter Rumball has mastered the art of Australian sparkling red wine. He led the renaissance of the style in the 1980s. The wine is made from Coonawarra, Barossa and McLaren Vale shiraz grapes by the méthode champenoise. This recipe was developed during many camping trips to the Northern Flinders Ranges on the edge of the true "outback" of South Australia. Red kangaroo curry can be made and left to cook on a very slow fire, to be ready on arrival back from a hard day's walking in rugged, magnificent country.

red kangaroo curry and sparkling shiraz
with basmati rice and sweet mango chutney

1 kg fresh kangaroo meat, medium cubed
1 tbsp Australian olive oil
2 medium onions, peeled and chopped
5 cloves of garlic, peeled and chopped
2 x 400 mL cans of good-quality coconut milk
1 tbsp fish sauce
1 tbsp soy sauce
3 cm finely sliced lemongrass stalk
(store lemongrass stalks in the freezer)
3 tbsp laksa paste
3 handfuls of fresh basil leaves
4 potatoes, washed and roughly cubed
2 carrots, broadly sliced on the angle
4 red capsicums, halved, de-seeded,
grilled skin side up, skinned and thick-sliced
10 medium mushrooms, cubed with stalks on
A few tbsp coconut powder
Dash of salt

cook and serve
Divide the kangaroo meat into thirds and brown each lot in hot oil in a camp oven. Remove the browned meat and rest. Add onion and garlic and fry until slightly caramelised. Return the rested meat. Add the coconut milk, fish sauce, soy sauce and lemongrass; then the laksa paste, basil, potato, carrot and capsicum. Cover and cook on low coals for a minimum of 1½ hours, with some coals on top. Add the mushrooms 30 minutes before serving, and thicken with coconut powder. Add salt, to taste. Cook on low coals for a further 20 minutes.

Serve with steamed basmati rice, sweet mango chutney and a chilled glass of Peter Rumball sparkling shiraz.

manfredi's comment
Lean and tasty, kangaroo
is perfectly suited to this
slow-cooked curry. Not only will
it retain its own distinctive flavour,
but take on those wonderful flavours
of spices and coconut milk.
The complexity of aged shiraz
coupled with the winemaking
finesse in Peter's Australian
classic is more than a match
for the heat of the curry.

109

ralph fowler wines

Mount Benson

Following a highly acclaimed winemaking career extending over three decades, Ralph Fowler now pursues his belief in the potential of the recently developed Mount Benson area. In 1998, Ralph and his wife Deborah established their own vineyard on this part of the Limestone Coast. They were attracted to its terrain, weather and, most of all, the limestone soils.

Ralph Fowler Wines prides itself on utilising the very latest environmentally friendly viticultural techniques. The winery is also ultra-modern, although the winemaking philosophy is traditional and non-interventionist, enabling it to capture both regional and varietal purity in all its wines.

fresh crayfish and chilled late-picked semillon
with avocado & spanish-onion salsa

2 kg freshly cooked crayfish
Mixed salad leaves, Viva extra virgin olive oil,
lime juice and cracked pepper, to serve

salsa
1 avocado, finely diced
1 medium Spanish onion, finely chopped
Juice of 1 lime
Freshly ground black pepper
and sea salt, to taste

prepare and serve
Remove crayfish tail meat in one piece.
Slice into medallions. Combine all salsa ingredients.

To serve, centre salad leaves on plate, top with crayfish medallions, drizzle with olive oil and lime juice and add cracked pepper to taste. Surround with salsa. Serve with chilled late-picked semillon.

manfredi's comment

The southern crayfish is one of the finest-eating crustaceans in the world. Treating it this way, simply boiled in well salted water and served with avocado, some red onion and dressed with extra virgin olive oil and a splash of lime, gives the flesh a lift without overwhelming its delicate flavour. Late-picked semillon is perfect with the richness of crayfish flesh.

ravenswood lane

Adelaide Hills

Conceived in France and created in the Adelaide Hills by John and Helen Edwards, Ravenswood Lane wines are neither European nor Australian in style, but rather the best of both worlds.

John describes his wine as:
stylish – an evolutionary new style;
offering synergy with food;
slippery and sensuous;
delivers in the mouth;
powerful but fine;
an "occasion" wine.

These wines have the structure and finesse of Europe's best, complemented by intense flavours and spice, thanks to Australian sunlight and the terroir of Ravenswood Lane.

moroccan lamb and shiraz
with baked potatoes and green salad

Leg of lamb
2 tbsp fresh lemon juice
Juice of 1 small lime
2 large cloves of garlic, finely chopped
1 knob of ginger, finely chopped
1 cup mint leaves, chopped
1 tbsp each ground cumin
and ground coriander seeds
4 tbsp extra virgin olive oil
1 tsp cayenne pepper
2 tsp paprika

marinate the lamb
Mix all other ingredients together and generously cover the leg of lamb. Refrigerate for 1-2 days in a closed container.

cook and serve
Preheat oven to 170ºC-180ºC. Cover lamb liberally with sea salt prior to cooking. Roast 15-17 minutes per 500 g lamb.

Serve with halved, oiled and salted potatoes baked in a very hot oven (220ºC), a green salad, and a glass of Ravenswood Lane Reunion shiraz.

manfredi's comment
The addition of Moroccan spices to the marinade taps into the intense fruit-and-spice combination of cooler-climate shiraz from the Adelaide Hills. The touch of mint is especially resonant.

113

rbj vintners

Barossa Valley

"Bruce" is the imaginary third party that provides the "B" for the title RBJ. Why the name Bruce was chosen, Russell Johnstone (the "J" of the group) explains, is because most Australian families have a "Bruce". Chris Ringland (the "R") completes this ensemble of passionate Barossa producers.

Since their foundation in 1991, RBJ Vintners have been forging a name for themselves on the strength of the big, flavoursome Barossa reds they create from very old vines. Their dedication to regional traditions, combined with large dollops of hard work, makes their future of excellence assured.

provençal onion tart and mourvèdre/grenache
with mixed green salad

8 large onions, thinly sliced
2 cloves of garlic, chopped
Extra virgin olive oil
Fresh herbs tied into 2 bunches
1 uncooked 23-25 cm round of pizza dough
Handful of pitted black olives
Sea salt and pepper
Mixed green salad, to serve

cook and serve
Cook onions and garlic in a small drizzle of the oil. Add one of the bunches of herbs. Cook slowly until onions melt down. Remove herbs and cool. Cover dough base with onion mixture, and olives. Strip leaves from the second bunch of herbs, chop and sprinkle on the tart. Season and bake in a very hot oven (230°C) for 20-25 minutes.

Serve hot or cold, with a mixed green salad and a glass of RBJ.

manfredi's comment

The sweet, caramelised flavours of the onions and garlic are achieved by cooking them slowly at low temperature. The result is an almost jam-like consistency, perfect as topping, and balancing the tangy black olives. Be sure to roll the base nice and thin, and accompany the tart with soft, mouth-filling RBJ.

Left: Russell Johnstone, Lynette Collins and their daughter, Nathalie

rockford wines

Barossa Valley

Robert O'Callaghan is a passionate and driven man. In the mid-1980s he played a crucial role in preserving some plots of century-old, dry-farmed shiraz vines threatened by a vine-pull scheme. Robert utilises the fruit from these treasured vines to make one of Australia's most sought-after wines – the super-concentrated Basket Press shiraz. This legend is created with restored winery equipment that is even older than the vines!

Robert makes the most of the South Australian outback. He thoroughly enjoys slipping off into the bush and whipping up a feast of local produce, accompanied by his hand-made wines to share with family and friends.

camp oven lamb and basket press shiraz
with roasted vegetables

take with you
1 slice of Australian outback
1 fresh and beautiful water view
1 bunch of friends
1 box of crystal glasses
1 camp oven
1 safe picnic fire
Lamb and vegetables
Several bottles of great wine

rule of the day
Take your time. Enjoy the wine as much as the food and put out the fire before you go home.

manfredi's comment
This is typical of Robert's
understated style. Just look
at all those caramelised
vegetables and the succulent,
rosemary-scented lamb.
To get the best out of this
dish, make sure the vegetables
are cut into rough chunks,
and use either shoulder or
leg of lamb for maximum
juiciness. Perfect with
Basket Press shiraz.

*Above: Tom Ramsay, Pam O'Donnell
and Robert O'Callaghan*

rusden wines

Barossa Valley

Dennis Canute and his wife Christine have owned and nurtured their vineyard, located in the Vine Vale area on the gentle slopes of the eastern Barossa, for the past two decades. Their son Christian lends his winemaking talent to the family venture.

Together the team handcraft bold, fruit-driven wines. Their Black Guts Shiraz is one of those. It oozes rich berry fruit and spice characters and the mouth-feel is sappy, soft and warming. Christian's wife Amy Loechel is an artist who creates the labels for Rusden. Perhaps one day their baby daughter Cadell will represent the third generation of vigneron!

kangaroo fillet and shiraz
with mustard sauce and caesar salad

¹/₂ cup chopped basil
¹/₄ cup red wine
2 tbsp seeded mustard
¹/₂ cup soy sauce
4 tbsp kecap manis
3 cloves of garlic, crushed
500 g saddle fillet of kangaroo
Olive oil
Caesar salad and crusty bread, to serve
Sprigs of fennel, to garnish

prepare, cook and serve
Mix basil, wine, mustard, soy sauce, kecap manis and garlic. Marinate kangaroo in this mixture for 2-3 hours. Drain, reserving marinade. Seal meat on char-grill. Lower heat and baste with oil while cooking to your taste. Do not overcook. Stand for a few minutes before carving. Add I cup water to reserved marinade and boil down to a thin sauce consistency.

Serve kangaroo with sauce, caesar salad and crusty bread, and garnish with fennel. Accompany with Rusden shiraz.

manfredi's comment
Kangaroo fillet should be cooked rare to medium-rare for maximum flavour and tenderness. It's a flesh that has little fat through it, so that if it is overcooked it becomes dry and stringy. It's no coincidence some of the best 'roo dishes in the country come from the Barossa, the same area that produces some of the best shiraz.

Left: Christian Canute, Amy Loechel, and their daughter, Cadell

schild estate wines

Barossa Valley

Ed Schild established his first small vineyard in Barossa's south in 1952. His landholdings increased over time and he now has the largest area of privately owned vineyards in the region. Initially Ed sold his grapes to other producers, but in 1998 he released the first wines bearing the Schild name and hasn't looked back. Exceptional fruit quality and regional definition throughout the range are the hallmarks of these award-winning wines.

Daniel Eggleton manages the public relations and cellar door of the estate. His days are busy, so his favourite lunch is quick and easy to prepare, assembled from fresh local produce.

antipasto platter and cabernet sauvignon
with maggie beer's capsicum pâté and farm follies chutney

Maggie Beer's capsicum pâté
Farm Follies chutney
Smoked ham
Prosciutto
Smoked turkey
Metwurst
Artichoke hearts
Spring onions
Dill cucumbers
Sun-dried tomatoes
Roasted eggplant
Stuffed olives
Aged cheddar
Brie
Fresh, crusty bread

assemble and serve
Keep all foods cold until 30 minutes before serving. Arrange in an enticing display on platters or large plates, provide plenty of fresh, sliced bread, and have a bottle of wine and glasses at the ready!

manfredi's comment
The antipasto has been adopted by
Australians as the perfect casual way
to eat. It is used to tease and tantalise
the palate by offering a variety of different
tastes. It can be laboriously elaborate
or simple and understated, but the
antipasto should always have
seduction as its goal.

Left: Daniel Eggleton

simon hackett wines

McLaren Vale

Simon is the fourth generation of the Hackett family to be involved in agricultural pursuits in South Australia, and his father was a graduate of the inaugural oenology course at the esteemed Roseworthy College in 1938. Simon began his career in winemaking at the age of 18, serving his apprenticeship at Saltram Winery in the Barossa Valley under the watchful eye of master winemaker Peter Lehmann. He gained further experience in the winemaking team headed by Grant Burge at Southern Vales Winery (now Tatachilla Wines) in McLaren Vale.

In 1984, Simon established his own winery in a disused cellar on a hill overlooking the beautiful countryside of McLaren Vale. Here, he produces a range of rich, bold and innovative wines using grapes grown in the McLaren Vale, Barossa Valley and Adelaide Hills regions of South Australia.

loin lamb racks (jumbucks) and shiraz
with pumpkin mash and caramelised onions

8 loin lamb racks (2 per person)
20 g dried rosemary leaves
80 g shaved honey ham, chopped
Virgin olive oil
Pumpkin mash and caramelised
onions, to serve

prepare, cook and serve
Trim lamb and cut pockets in the underside of the chops. Pack with rosemary, then ham, then rosemary again. Preheat a heavy baking dish. Lightly season the lamb and drizzle oil over. Bake at 240ºC for 20 minutes, then reduce to 200ºC for 30 minutes.

Serve with pumpkin mash and caramelised onions; and, if desired, baby beetroot, parsnip chips, steamed fresh asparagus tips and mint jelly. Accompany with Simon Hackett shiraz.

manfredi's comment
I can conjure the smell and taste of the roast lamb and rosemary, because it's part of my childhood. I can also smell and taste McLaren Vale shiraz and, with roast lamb, there's no better combination.

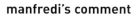

tapestry wines

McLaren Vale

The name Tapestry was chosen to encapsulate the philosophy of weaving the threads of viticulture and oenology together, to create a work of art.

This beautiful estate winery is surrounded by one of its vineyards. It is situated in the middle of the McLaren Vale region and offers sweeping views of the area, giving inspiration to winemaker Jon Ketley. Tapestry's highly prized other vineyard is located at Bakers Gully, an elevated site in the northeast corner of the region.

Owner Robert Gerard (a visionary and staunch advocate of all things South Australian) purchased the company in 1997 in order to continue showcasing the pure regional characteristics that are the hallmark of the Tapestry style.

salt & pepper king george whiting fillets and riesling

with salsa and riesling glaze

1 bottle riesling
1 tbsp sugar
1 avocado
1 red onion
1 mango
10 cherry tomatoes
2 corn cobs
Extra virgin olive oil
8 King George whiting fillets
1 cup cornflour
1 cup plain flour
1 tbsp each salt and pepper
1 tbsp five-spice powder
500 mL peanut oil
Prawn crisps, to serve

the performance
Make a glaze by boiling the riesling with the sugar until reduced by half. Dice avocado, onion and mango. Halve tomatoes, cut corn from cobs, add a little oil and mix all into a salsa.

Remove skins from fish fillets. Combine flours, salt, pepper and five-spice. Dip fillets into flour mix, then fry in hot peanut oil. Remove fish, pour off oil, add glaze to the pan and boil hard for a few minutes, stirring and scraping brown bits from pan.

Call your guests to the table! Spoon riesling glaze over the fish, garnish with prawn crisps and serve with salsa and another bottle of riesling.

Above: Jon Ketley

manfredi's comment

King George whiting is one of the best eating fish in Australia, with its delicate, finely flaked texture and pearly white flesh. Lightly spiced and then fried to a crispy texture, it is ideal when washed down with a tangy, fresh McLaren Vale riesling.

125

turkey flat vineyards

Barossa Valley

Peter Schulz is a fourth-generation Barossa grape-grower and, along with his wife Christie, owns and operates the Turkey Flat vineyards and winery. Shiraz vines were planted on the property by one of the first Barossa settlers, Silesian migrant Johann Friedrich August Fielder, in 1847. Peter's ancestors bought the property in the early 1860s and continued with the vineyard, as well as starting a prosperous butcher's business.

The butcher shop and original cellar are now part of the winery and cellar door, and the antique vines provide the rich, compact fruit for which the Turkey Flat reds are renowned.

One of the flagship reds, the Butchers Block, is a blend of mataro, shiraz and grenache. It abounds with super-concentrated, spicy redcurrant fruit flavours, which burst in the mouth and seem to linger forever.

rabbit casserole and mataro/shiraz/grenache
with cannellini beans

1.5 kg farmed Barossa rabbit,
cut into six (discard ribs)
125 g Linkes smoked Barossa meaty speck
2 cloves of garlic, crushed
2 tsp smoked paprika
1/4 cup extra virgin olive oil
250 mL Turkey Flat mataro/shiraz/grenache
1/2 cup cannellini beans, soaked
overnight in water
2 x 400 g cans chopped tomatoes
150 g salted Barossa black olives,
soaked overnight in water
2 cups water
Green salad and crusty bread, to serve

cook and serve
Brown rabbit and speck separately in an oiled pan and place in a casserole dish. Add garlic, paprika and oil to the pan. Stir. Deglaze with a little wine. Add remaining wine and boil. Add the wine mixture, drained beans, tomatoes, olives and water to casserole. Cover and bake for 2 1/2 hours. Serve with green salad, crusty bread and a glass of Turkey Flat red blend.

manfredi's comment
This is rabbit at its best. It's a flesh that takes on the nuances of its accompaniments as well as retaining its distinctive personality. Here there are flavours of speck and spicy paprika, as well as tangy olives, all held together with rich Barossa red.

whisson lake

Adelaide Hills

Whisson Lake is unusual in that it produces just one wine – pinot noir. The vineyard is also the highest and steepest in the area, features that provide the long growing season and ideal exposure for making rich, complex pinot noir.

Initially, fruit from the vineyard was sold to other wine companies. In 1992 the Whisson and Lake families decided to produce a wine in order to negotiate better grape prices. The resulting pinot noir, with its intensity, spiciness and focused structure, gave the Whisson Lake team the confidence to pursue winemaking seriously.

Mark Whisson also takes his cars seriously. In his spare time, he competes in classic and historic rallies. He likens his Porsche to a great pinot noir – aristocratic and stylish. Mark and chef Ian Burrows planned a similarly stylish dish to match this complex wine.

braised pig's trotters and pinot noir
with a farce of chicken and goose-liver confit

4 pig's back trotters
100 g carrots, sliced
100 g white onions, sliced
100 g celery, sliced
150 mL dry white wine
2 tbsp white port
250 mL brown veal stock
1 chicken breast, cooked and puréed
50 g goose-liver confit
1 egg white
200 mL thick cream
2 tbsp Italian parsley
Tarragon and chervil, finely chopped
Sea salt and freshly ground white pepper, to taste

cook and serve
Braise trotters covered, at 170ºC with all the vegetables, wine, port and stock for 3 hours, adding a little water from time to time if mixture begins to dry out. Cool trotters and discard vegetables. Open trotters out flat and place on foil. Stuff each with mixture of puréed chicken, goose liver, egg white, cream, herbs and seasonings. Roll trotters up tightly in the foil. Chill for 3 hours. Serve with warm lentils and wilted baby spinach, plus the essential glass of pinot noir.

manfredi's comment
Rich, unctuous and complex, this is a dish that needs wine of structure and balance. The pig's trotters provide a deliciously gelatinous, sticky wrapping for the luscious, creamy farce. Cool-climate Adelaide Hills pinot noir is the perfect foil.

Left: Mark Whisson with his beloved 1973 Porsche 911 2.7RS

victoria
and
tasmania

Victoria's various climatic regions are not only suitable for a broad range of wine styles, but also a vast array of fresh vegetable and herb gardens. Such botanical treasure troves can be found in the backyards of countless residential blocks in Melbourne's suburbia, as well as in the boutique vineyards of Victoria.

Many of those gardens are testament to a European heritage. The freshness and variety of their produce are essential to the dinner table and, of course, the delicious vegetables accompany the wonderful wines made to go with them.

These home-grown vegetable and herb gardens are full of colour and variety. Juicy, rosy red tomatoes, fresh green and red radicchio, green and yellow-striped zucchini, and shiny yellow and red capsicums lead the parade.

Part of the tradition at The Green Vineyards is to preserve those wonderful fresh flavours. An annual ritual is to grow and harvest fresh tomatoes and make numerous bottles of pure tomato purée sauce. This serves as a basis for many dishes, such as pizza. Basil is added to infuse its aromatic flavours into the sauce, which is then stored in those classic beer bottles and used all year round. Buon appetito!

home-made tomato sauce

5 kg ripe tomatoes
2 tbsp salt
1 large bunch of fresh basil leaves

Boil the tomatoes in a large tub of salted water. Boil 7-10 minutes or until the skins break. Remove from water, then strain and cool. Remove the skins and seeds either by hand or with a machine that can be purchased from a specialist cookware shop. Blend the tomato pulp and pour through a small funnel into beer bottles that have first been thoroughly cleaned and dried.

Place 1 basil leaf into each bottle of sauce, before sealing with crown seals. Stand the bottles upright in a large pot of boiling water and boil gently for 1 hour.

Sergio Carlie
The Green Vineyards, Port Phillip, Vic

Victoria

all saints estate
balgownie estate
chambers rosewood winery
chrismont wines
dal zotto wines
delatite winery
elmswood estate
gapsted wines
goulburn valley estate wines
knight granite hills wines
massoni homes
mount avoca vineyard
paringa estate
pizzini wines
stanton & killeen wines
the green vineyards

all saints estate

Rutherglen

A majestic fortress lined with century-old elm trees emerges from the countryside after a 3½ hour drive northeast from Melbourne. Despite its imposing façade, the welcome to All Saints Estate couldn't be warmer, nor the hospitality friendlier.

All Saints Estate is owned by Peter Brown, the fourth generation of the well-known Victoria-based winemaking family. His lifetime of experience in the wine industry is reflected in the way he oversees all operations in the vineyard, winery, restaurant and bustling cellar door with meticulous care, yet soft-spoken ease. In addition to his vast wine-industry background, he also shares the Brown family traits of being convivial and affable, characteristics from which every visitor to the winery benefits.

roasted venison and durif
with angelhair pasta, local walnuts and game jus

4 x 180 g venison porterhouse steaks
12 juniper berries, bruised
1 tsp freshly cracked pepper
8 sprigs of fresh thyme
Vegetable oil
200 g mixed game bones
200 g mixed game trimmings, chopped
400 g mirepoix (equal quantities chopped
carrot, onion, celery and leek)
4 cloves of garlic
1 cup tomato paste
11 bay leaves
10 peppercorns
Knob of butter
500 mL red wine
3 tbsp redcurrant jelly
Salt
Angelhair pasta
1 bunch shallots, peeled
2 extra cloves of garlic, chopped
½ cup walnut pieces
A little extra red wine, for deglazing
Milawa blue cheese
Chopped parsley

prepare, cook and serve
Marinate steak in berries, pepper, thyme
and oil to cover.

Roast bones and trimmings in hot oven with mirepoix, garlic, tomato paste, bay leaves, peppercorns and butter. Add red wine and reduce to half. Simmer, adding a little water from time to time if needed, for a few hours, then strain into a clean pot. Simmer the mixture until it is a sticky, rich game jus, then add jelly and season.

Salt and seal steaks on hot grill, then roast in a very hot oven (230°C) for 3 minutes, for rare. Rest meat in a warm place. Cook pasta, and sauté shallots, garlic and walnuts in a little oil. Remove these, deglaze pan with extra wine, and add to the jus. Toss hot pasta with Milawa blue cheese and a touch of parsley.

Serve steaks with pasta, walnut mixture and jus. Enjoy with a glass of the lusty durif.

manfredi's comment
The durif grape produces a big wine
and it needs big flavours to accompany it.
The red-wine reduction with the redcurrant
jelly works very nicely here with rare
grilled venison, the angelhair pasta
providing respite from the richness.

balgownie estate

Bendigo

The original 13 hectares of vines planted at the Maiden Gully site in 1969 provide the foundation for the delectable reds produced by Balgownie, which was one of the first wine businesses founded in this gold-mining area. Over the years, the estate earned its reputation with the production of powerful, flavoursome reds that live happily in the cellar... that is, if you can resist drinking them!

Tobias Ansted is Balgownie's talented and highly motivated winemaker. He is concentrating on further enhancing the quality and reputation of the Balgownie Estate wines, particularly the shiraz and cabernet sauvignon. He is keen to indulge his passion for the French wine region of Burgundy – where he has worked vintages – by continuing to make small quantities of chardonnay and pinot noir.

roasted quail and shiraz
with chicken liver stuffing and shiraz jus

1 knob of butter
20 mL virgin olive oil
1 brown onion and 4 spring onions, finely chopped
2 cloves of garlic, chopped
250 g organic chicken livers, chopped
1 sprig fresh tarragon
1/2 cup chopped parsley
100 g shelled walnuts
Salt and pepper, to taste
4 quails (deboned)
4 strips of prosciutto
Seasonal winter vegetables, to serve

Heat butter and oil. Fry onions and garlic gently until clear. Add livers and cook until they change colour. Add herbs, walnuts and seasonings. Use this mixture to stuff the quails. Wrap quails in prosciutto and secure with a toothpick. Roast in a moderate oven (180°C) for 20 minutes.

shiraz jus
500 mL chicken stock
100 mL shiraz
2 tbsp brown sugar
2 sprigs fresh tarragon
Fresh cracked pepper
1 cup parsley, chopped

Simmer all jus ingredients except parsley until liquid is reduced by half. Add parsley and pour over the quail.

Serve with seasonal winter vegetables and a generous glass of Balgownie Estate shiraz.

manfredi's comments
The prosciutto here is a nice touch, as it protects the quail flesh, keeping it moist, and crisps up as it cooks. The addition of chicken livers gives the dish that little bit of extra richness – just the thing for shiraz. The hardest thing here is deboning the quail – perhaps you can ask your supplier to do it.

chambers rosewood winery

Rutherglen

As with any great story, there is a fascinating matrix of people, purpose and passion behind the protagonist, Bill Chambers. The Chambers family first planted vines in Rutherglen in the 1850s – a time when the area prospered in the gold rush. By the end of that century, the region (along with most of the vinous world) succumbed to the disastrous vine disease, phylloxera. For many, this epidemic signalled the end of grape-growing, but for the Chambers family it heralded the beginning of the production of a particular range of styles, including two of Australia's great wine gifts to the world – liqueur muscat and tokay.

Recently, the influential American wine writer Robert Parker awarded both Bill's Rare Tokay and his Rare Muscat 100 points from a possible 100! A sparsely granted accolade indeed – thus galvanising the international market for these unique Australian treasures. ("Rare" denotes that the wine's blended vintages exceed an average of 50 years of age.)

But Bill is a reluctant legend. The twinkle in his eye, his broad smile and ready wit never wane. Perhaps this is due to his prowess in preparing the quintessential recovery breakfast barbecue.

bbq bacon & eggs and botrytis tokay
with tomatoes, sausages and onions

Fresh farm eggs
Home-grown tomatoes
Top-quality sausages
Trimmed rashers of bacon
Sliced onions
Crusty toast

procedure
Invite friends over
for a "late-start"
weekend breakfast.
Dust off the apron.
Start up the BBQ.
Open the muscat and
have a hair of the dog.
Cook all ingredients
to your taste, and serve
with buttered toast
and more muscat.

manfredi's comment
What a great idea – Rutherglen
botrytis tokay with a lazy, late breakfast!
To be fair to one of the world's great
wines, be sure to have the best
free-range eggs, the best sausages
and the best bacon. This should
be a real treat.

141

chrismont wines

King Valley

When Arnie Pizzini completed his horticultural studies in 1980, he felt compelled to move back to the King Valley, the place where he grew up and where his family still grew grapes to establish his own vineyard. Arnie feels that he has wine coursing through his veins – he has a long-established heritage of grape-growing, originating from the Alto-Adige region of northern Italy.

Arnie believes in letting the grape speak for itself. This belief encapsulates his wines perfectly, as they shine with pristine, precise varietal characters. Their grace and subtlety of style are hightlighted in this delicious demonstration of wine and food matching!

whole deboned quail and pinot grigio
with light mustard cream sauce

1 carrot, 2 celery stalks,
1 leek, 5 cloves of garlic and
1 red capsicum, all finely chopped
1 knob of butter
20 mL olive oil
1 cup Italian parsley
2 cups coarse breadcrumbs
1 cup currants
500 mL chicken stock
1 cup pinot grigio
Salt and pepper, to taste
6 whole tunnel-boned quails
6 slices of prosciutto
Extra olive oil
Extra knob of butter
1 tbsp seeded mustard
250 mL King Island cream

prepare and cook
Reserve some of the vegetables (no capsicum) for the sauce. Fry remaining vegetables in butter and olive oil, until caramelised. Add parsley, breadcrumbs and currants. Moisten with half the chicken stock and a splash of wine. Season to taste. Stuff the quails until they regain natural shape. Cross the legs and push them into the opening until only the thighs are showing. Wrap with prosciutto. Drizzle extra oil over the quail and bake in a preheated 200ºC oven for about 15 minutes on the top shelf.

and quickly while the quail is cooking...
Gently fry the reserved vegetables in extra butter in a saucepan until soft but not brown. Add the remaining wine, and the mustard and cream. Simmer for 10 minutes to reduce. Add remaining stock. Pour over quail when serving. Serve with La Zona pinot grigio.

manfredi's comment
Italian cooking is not always olive-oil based. Arnie's recipe recalls the butter-based cuisine of the cooler far north of Italy. Still, simplicity is the key to all Italian cooking and the crisp flavours of pinot grigio are a nice foil for the full flavours of the mustard cream sauce. Down the road from Chrismont, at Milawa, comes some of the best mustard in the world.

dal zotto wines

King Valley

The King Valley was famous for tobacco cultivation until the decline of the industry in the late 1970s. This void in production left farmers (many of them Italian immigrants), searching for alternatives. Otto Dal Zotto decided to develop his love for traditional winemaking and, together with his family, planted French and Italian grape varieties on their farmlands. In 1994, Otto launched the Dal Zotto label.

Family is of great importance to the Dal Zottos and dinner, complete with home-made wines, is one of the most important times of the day.

Above: Otto Dal Zotto and his prized Harley Davidson

veal spezzatino and cabernet/merlot
with polenta di patate

veal spezzatino
3 tbsp olive oil
2 medium onions, chopped
1 kg beef or veal, cubed
2 tbsp tomato paste
1/2 cup of red wine
Sage, oregano and 2 bay leaves
2 sticks celery
2 large carrots
4 cloves of garlic, crushed
450 g can crushed tomatoes

Heat olive oil and sauté onion. Add meat and brown well. Add tomato paste and red wine. Allow juices to reduce. Combine herbs, vegetables and tomatoes and stir. Add water, to cover. Cover with lid and simmer for 2 1/2 hours, either on the stove-top or in the oven.

polenta di patate
1 kg potatoes
2 tbsp salt
1 1/2 cups plain flour
1 3/4 cups polenta
8 cloves of garlic, crushed
2 tbsp butter
1/2 large onion, thinly sliced

Boil potatoes in salted water until soft, then mash well. Mix flour, polenta and garlic together. Return mashed potatoes to stove and stir in polenta mixture. Whisk well and lower the heat. In a small saucepan, heat butter and sauté onion. Add onion to polenta mixture and stir every 3-5 minutes until smooth. Continue for 30-40 minutes, until firm.

Pour polenta into a low, wide dish or onto a board, slice, and serve with veal spezzatino and a generous glass of cabernet/merlot.

manfredi's comment
As this casserole requires prolonged cooking of the meat, it's a good idea to use a cut of veal that retains moisture and becomes tender when slow-cooked. Brisket is good, as well as veal breast. The unusual accompaniment of potato polenta makes this quite a rich, cold-weather dish, perfect for a rich cabernet merlot.

Above: Otto and his wife, Elena, his sons Simon and Michael, and his mother, Maria

Left: Elena Dal Zotto

145

delatite winery

Victorian High Country

Grape-growing was far from the minds of the Ritchie family when they were raising cattle and growing crops in the Victorian High Country. This had been the family concern for more than 150 years, and not until 1970 did they turn to grape and wine production. This shift in focus came about when Robert Ritchie went skiing on nearby Mount Buller and met a winemaker who told him of the potential of his family's steep hillside property for growing premium grapes. The rest is history!

To the casual observer, it seemed unlikely that grapes could grow and ripen successfully in such bitter conditions. However, Robert and his wife Vivienne took the winemaker's advice. They demonstrated that the long growing season of this marginal climate is, in fact, ideal for cultivating flavoursome, ripe grapes. Their daughter Rosalind is now their winemaker and son David, the viticulturist.

Above: Robert Ritchie and daughter Rosalind inspect the vines

baked mountain-river trout and gewürztraminer
with ginger, chilli and delatite dressing

1 cup jasmine rice
3-4 tbsp shredded fresh ginger
Juice and zest of 2 limes
5 small red chillies, chopped
1/2 onion, finely chopped and lightly
fried in peanut oil
4 small trout, cleaned and scaled
1 tbsp peanut oil and 1 tbsp oriental
sesame oil, mixed together
Pinch of salt
1 tsp brown sugar
1 tbsp fresh ginger juice
1 1/2 tbsp sesame oil
Steamed bok choy and chilli jam,
to serve

**For a chilli jam recipe,
see Bimbadgen Estate, pp22-23.**

prepare and cook the trout
Cook the rice in salted water. Drain. Add ginger, half the lime juice, lime zest, half the chopped chilli and the fried onion. Preheat oven to 200ºC. Wash and dry the trout. Stuff with rice mixture. Lightly brush both sides of fish with peanut and sesame oil mixture. Season with salt, to taste. Bake fish uncovered for 12 minutes, or until just cooked.

make the delatite dressing
Combine remaining lime juice with brown sugar, remaining chilli, ginger juice and sesame oil.

Serve trout with bok choy, chilli jam, Delatite dressing, and the mandatory gewürztraminer!

manfredi's comment
Gewürtztraminer really shines
with the assertive flavours of chilli,
lime and ginger. Add to this the
wonderfully earthy flavour of
roasted freshly caught river trout,
and we have a great example of
contemporary Australian cooking.

147

elmswood estate

Yarra Valley

The reason Dianne Keller and her husband Rod set up their own wine business was that they knew "...It was time!" Living in the heart of Melbourne had not turned out to be the ideal lifestyle choice. So, when they fell instantly in love with a vineyard property on the southern side of the Yarra Valley and settled there in 1999, they did so with the intention of making their own wine and launching their own label.

Fortunately, Rod and Dianne knew that running their own wine business was not all about wandering aimlessly through the vineyard with a financial newspaper in one hand and a glass of champagne in the other! The challenges of their hard work have had their rewards, as Elmswood's wines are well made and display clean, crisp flavours – perfect when paired with up-tempo foods.

linguine and chardonnay
with prosciutto, spinach and feta

500 g linguine
3 tbsp extra virgin olive oil
1 tbsp grated lime zest
4 tbsp lime juice
2 cloves of garlic, crushed
1 red chilli, seeded and finely chopped
3 tbsp capers
10 slices prosciutto
200 g baby English spinach leaves, chopped
200 g feta cheese marinated in herbs and oil
4 lightly poached quail eggs, to serve

Cook pasta until al dente. Drain. While pasta is cooking, heat oil over medium heat. Add zest, lime juice, garlic, chilli, capers and prosciutto. Cook, stirring. Toss spinach and feta cheese through the pasta.

serve
Top each serving with quail eggs. Serve with a flavoursome cool-climate chardonnay.

manfredi's comment
This is very much a modern Australian pasta composition, but be careful with the chilli, as too much can kill a wine. For a texture contrast, try frying the prosciutto first in a little olive oil, then crumbling it over the pasta before serving.

149

gapsted wines

Victorian High Country

Gapsted winery is situated near the popular Victorian ski fields. Its wines capture the essence of the cool alpine influence in their potent, yet precise, fruit flavours.

Successful grape-growing in such a chilly climate is a tricky affair. Techniques that offer maximum exposure to sunlight and circulation of air throughout the vine are, therefore, essential. Gapsted's chief executive, Shayne Cunningham, and winemaker, Michael Cope-Williams, have the perfect solution to ensure maximum-quality grapes. The "Ballerina" system of canopy control (the canopy is the vine's fruit-bearing structure) allows gentle morning sun and soft mountain breezes to delicately ripen fruit, giving vibrant colours and lip-smacking fruit flavours. So enamoured are they of the Ballerina system, they have not only named a range of Gapsted wines after it, but the winery's labels also proudly display it!

duo of trevally & salmon and chardonnay
with mushroom risotto and basil beurre blanc

risotto
1/2 white onion, chopped
1 tbsp vegetable oil
60 g button mushrooms, chopped finely
1/2 cup arborio rice
11/4 cups fish stock, mixed with
15 mL Asian fish sauce

mushroom cream
8 oyster mushrooms, sliced
1 cup cream
Salt and pepper, to taste

basil beurre blanc
2 shallots, finely chopped
150 mL white wine
200 g unsalted butter, diced and chilled
2-3 basil leaves, finely sliced
1 tbsp lemon juice
Salt and pepper

fish
80 g trevally
80 g salmon

make the risotto
Cook onion in oil in a heavy pan. Add mushrooms and cook until soft. Add rice. Stir 1 minute. Add boiling stock. Cook on low heat for 15 minutes until still slightly crunchy.

mushroom cream
Simmer all ingredients together for 5 minutes.

basil beurre blanc
Simmer shallots and wine until reduced by half. Over low heat, add butter, piece by piece. When almost melted, remove. Stir and add basil and lemon juice. Season to taste.

cook the fish
Sauté fish in a non-stick pan, or grill 3 minutes each side.

now, the triumph!
Bring mushroom cream to the boil and add risotto. Allow to absorb. Arrange fish fillets on top of risotto, spoon basil beurre blanc onto the plate, and garnish as desired. Serve with a flavoursome cool-climate chardonnay.

manfredi's comment
This method of making risotto is quite recent in Italy and was developed by Gualtiero Marchesi. He calls it *risotto mantecato* – risotto mounted with butter. It gives a really creamy, "wet" risotto. Delicious with Gapsted's fine, rich Ballerina chardonnay.

Left: Shayne Cunningham and Michael Cope-Williams

151

goulburn valley estate wines

Goulburn Valley

When Rocky Scarpari took his wife Mary and their young family on a trip to his childhood home – Calabria in southern Italy – their lives changed. Being back among the large oak barrels and breathing in the aromas of the family winery, he was filled with happy memories of helping to make the wine.

With Rocky's passion for winemaking reignited, the family set up their own small vineyard and winery in the Goulburn Valley in 1999. Growing grapes is not far removed from Rocky's former role of cultivating fruit and vegetables, and the Scarparis still take tremendous care of their own orchard and vegetable garden.

mussels, scallops and sauvignon blanc
with spaghetti

2 kg mussels
1 tbsp extra virgin olive oil
2 cloves of garlic, chopped
1 onion, chopped
2 hot chillies, chopped
250 mL white wine
1 kg scallops
500 g spaghetti
Torn parsley and grated parmesan cheese, to garnish

prepare and cook
Wash and clean beards from mussels. Drain. Using a non-stick pan, add oil and heat. Add garlic, onion and chilli to pan. Stir until lightly browned. Add white wine and mussels. Cover and cook for 10 minutes on medium to high heat. Remove mussels from pan and stir in scallops. Cook on low heat until tender. Return mussel mixture again to heat. Cook spaghetti until al dente and drain.

To serve, arrange seafood on the spaghetti and garnish with parsley and parmesan cheese. Serve with chilled sauvignon blanc.

Right: Mary Scarpari

manfredi's comment
I love pasta prepared like this.
It has the big flavours of the Italian
Mediterranean, combined with
sparkling fresh Australian seafood.
This dish can take as much chilli
as you and your guests can handle,
because sauvignon blanc doesn't
mind a little heat. Try the dish
without parmesan first.

knight granite hills wines

Macedon Ranges

In 1970, the Knight family pioneered wine-growing in the Macedon Ranges when they established their vineyard on a property featuring majestic granite outcrops. To most, this unforgiving cold-climate setting would seem a highly unlikely spot to attempt to ripen grapes. The Knights' belief in the potential of the area, combined with their hard work towards maximising fruit quality, has paid off handsomely. Their award-winning wines abound with delicate, juicy and ripe fruit.

Here the winemaking is truly a family affair. Llew Knight makes the wines while his father, Gordon, looks after the vineyard, and Llew's mother, Heather, greets customers with a friendly smile at the cellar door.

Above: Llew Knight

fresh oysters and riesling
the traditional match!

Fresh oysters are divine with riesling... and never better than with Llew's riesling. In fact there is possibly no other wine that fits the bill. Vodka, however is also a traditional and most refreshing partner, especially when combined with tomato juice and a dash of Tabasco sauce in a shot glass.

This boutique winery is situated on the Burke and Wills Track in the Central Victoria wine region. On the day of our scheduled shoot our photographer, Oliver Strewe, became irretrievably lost somewhere along the track. Defeated and sympathetic to Burke and Wills' plight, Oliver reached for his 21st-century navigational device – the mobile phone – and drove through the winery gate as the sun was setting.

Several beers and five oyster/vodka shots on, the joys of excellent wines were all but forgotten as the winemaker and the photographer sat on the verandah, watching the moon rise over the vineyards.

manfredi's comment
With this wonderfully intense and
steely riesling, try getting as many
different oysters as possible. You'll
find that Pacific oysters, as well as
Sydney Rocks, will have different
flavours depending on where they
are grown. This little game is
a taste treat.

massoni homes

Mornington Peninsula

Restaurateur Leon Massoni originally established Main Creek Vineyard, and in 1995, the Home family purchased the property and wine company. As founder of Yellowglen, Ian Home felt naturally drawn to the region's cool climate, in which pinot noir and chardonnay grapes provide the elements of finely crafted sparkling wine. With this venture, however, Ian focused on developing beautiful table wines that exude personality and finesse.

The demand Ian has generated for the limited volume of his distinguished Massoni wines inspired him to start a second label – Homes – for those who missed out. And, as his culinary philosophy "Cook with the best and drink the rest" would suggest, Ian doesn't believe in missing out on anything!

bbq lamb fillets and pinot noir
with rosemary & pinot marinade

150 mL pinot noir
Splash of olive oil
2 garlic cloves, crushed and chopped
Fresh rosemary, snipped
Ground black pepper
18 baby lamb fillets or 6 lamb backstraps
(3 fillets or 1 backstrap per person)
Baked vegetables, to serve

marinate and cook
Combine the first 5 ingredients to make a marinade. Add lamb. Refrigerate overnight. Drain, dry and cook quickly on a BBQ, turning once.

To serve, place the lamb on a warm platter surrounded with baked vegetables. If using the larger backstraps, slice diagonally before serving. Make sure that you add rosemary to the oil when baking the vegetables. Serve with Ian Home's pinot noir.

manfredi's comment
I can smell the combination of the meat
and marinade sizzling to caramelised
perfection as little finger-length fillets
hit the hot barbecue plate. Leave the fillets
medium-rare as they are very tender, and
rest for a few moments before serving.

*Left: Ian Home in the barrel room with Delyse Graham,
Massoni Homes marketing manager*

mount avoca vineyard

Pyrenees

The Pyrenees has emerged as one of the premium wine-growing regions in the country. John Barry planted his vines in 1970 in the foothills of the Pyrenees Mountains, with the intention of fostering a second career to escape the bustle of city life.

Mount Avoca vineyard now ranks as the second oldest in the region and is planted with a broad spectrum of varieties. The area's mild climate and dry conditions result in the production of wines displaying intensity, yet fruit-flavour finesse.

Second-generation winemaker Matthew Barry, a qualified microbiologist from Monash University, ensures that the traditional family ideals of quality and purity are present through his hands-on approach from vineyard to bottle.

roasted duck and cabernet sauvignon
with chestnut stuffing and mulberry/cabernet jus

2 medium onions, sliced
1 tbsp butter
1 tbsp extra virgin olive oil
2 tbsp honey
200 g chestnuts, roasted (see below), shelled and chopped
1 small sprig fresh sage, chopped
1 medium duck
2 cups fresh mulberries
2 glasses Mount Avoca cabernet
Sage and rocket leaves, to garnish

note from the winemaker/cook:
Roasting chestnuts is easy. Simply score the top of each nut with a sharp knife – a little criss-cross usually does the trick – and place on a shallow tray in a very hot oven (230ºC) for 15 minutes. Cool and peel.

prepare and serve
Caramelise the onions in hot butter and oil, adding honey as you stir. Add chestnut flesh and half the sage, then cool. Mix well and stuff into the duck's cavity. Preheat the oven to 200ºC and bake for 30 minutes, then reduce to 180ºC for a further 60 minutes. Make the jus by combining the mulberries with 1 generous glass of cabernet. Simmer for 30 minutes until slightly syrupy, with a glass of wine in one hand and a wooden spoon in the other!

Serve the duck with the jus, and garnish with sage and rocket leaves. Accompany with a bottle of cabernet.

manfredi's comment
Just a note about seasonality here – it's probably easier to keep some chestnuts in the freezer and wait until mulberries come into season in spring, for this dish. The mulberry-and-cabernet sauce with duck is an inspired choice!

Left: Matthew Barry and his son, Flynn

paringa estate

Mornington Peninsula

Paringa Estate's founder, Lindsay McCall, is passionate about pinot noir. The complex, spicy pinots he makes are known to send consumers and critics alike straight to wine heaven. In fact, they are some of the most sought-after and highly awarded pinots in the country.

Lindsay strongly asserts that the greatest wine comes from "the best-possible fruit you can grow". He is dedicated to his vineyards, ensuring his vines are set up to reap maximum rewards. The quality and personality of the ultra-premium fruit shines through all the Paringa wines, as Lindsay's winemaking philosophy is strictly non-interventionist.

Roses are traditionally grown in vineyards world-wide. In days gone by, prior to the technical revolution, roses were planted among the vines as an early indicator of the destructive fungal disease, powdery mildew. Paringa Estate continues this tradition, with beautiful results.

stuffed haunch of rabbit and pinot noir
with flageolet-bean braise

2 rabbit's hind legs
200 g minced rabbit
50 g chopped prunes
50 g chopped walnuts
100 g diced streaky bacon
1/2 small onion, diced and sautéed
in a little butter
5 g chopped sage, rosemary and thyme
Sea salt and cracked pepper
1 egg
2 slices bayonne ham
100 g caul fat
 2 L chicken stock

stuffed haunch of rabbit
Carefully debone legs. Open the flesh and flatten with a cleaver. Combine all remaining ingredients (except ham, caul fat and chicken stock) in a stainless-steel bowl. Pan-fry together for a few minutes and test seasoning. Stuff mixture into flattened leg and fold to seal. Wrap with ham and roll in caul fat, sealing the stuffing in as you go. Refrigerate for 1 hour. Gently brown on all sides. Place in saucepan, cover with chicken stock and poach for 45 minutes.

flageolet-bean braise
Sauté some winter vegetables and bacon, without colouring, in 50 mL olive oil and a knob of butter. Cover with 500 mL chicken stock, adding a splash of sherry vinegar, a pinch of thyme and 4 cloves of roasted garlic. Add 200 g flageolet beans (pre-soaked) and simmer for 1 hour.

manfredi's comment
What a sensational dish! Either
wild or farmed rabbit can be used
here. The difference is really in
flavour and texture. Farmed rabbit
has a finer flavour and juicier texture,
while wild rabbit is gamier, with
drier flesh. Whatever is used,
it will be perfect with a spicy,
tightly structured pinot noir.

pizzini wines

King Valley

Three generations of the Pizzini family work together in their wine, food and hospitality businesses to enhance the growing tourism industry in the King Valley. The family's first vineyard was established in 1978, and it was soon apparent that their various sites were ideally suited to growing emergent Italian varieties.

In 1994 Fred and Katrina Pizzini began crafting wines under the Pizzini Wines label and quickly earned a reputation for producing elegant styles true to their variety. An assortment of French and Italian classics are represented, including the northern-Italian king of grapes: nebbiolo. These varieties are dear to the family heritage, and explain their approach to winemaking.

For visitors, a sumptuous dinner at the Pizzinis' award-winning Mountainview Hotel in Whitfield is a must, especially when combined with a stay at Lana-Trento B&B at the vineyard.

pork & duck cassoulet and nebbiolo
with skorthalia

500 g dried haricot beans,
soaked in cold water for 2 hours
300 g pork belly
200 g fresh pork rind
200 g onions, sliced
2 medium leeks, chopped
6 cloves of garlic
Fresh thyme and bouquet garni
2 L chicken broth
500 g pork fillet
50 g goose fat
350 g salsiccia (Italian sausage), thickly sliced
Olive oil
300 g ripe tomatoes, diced
I whole duck in segments,
baked with garlic and thyme
Salt and pepper
3 tbsp breadcrumbs

cassoulet
Drain beans, place in a pot with pork belly, rind, onion, leek, garlic, thyme, bouquet garni and broth. Simmer 1¹/₂ hours. Brown pork fillet in goose fat. Brown salsiccia in oil. Layer bean mixture, tomato and all meats in a casserole dish, seasoning to taste. Cover with breadcrumbs. Bake in moderate oven 1¹/₂ hours.

skorthalia
Crush 5 cloves of garlic and ¹/₂ tsp salt in mortar and pestle. Combine with 5 mashed potatoes. Whip ¹/₂ cup olive oil and ¹/₃ cup lemon juice alternately into the mash. Fold through ¹/₂ cup milk and ¹/₂ cup chopped parsley. Add seasoning.

Serve cassoulet and skorthalia with a good red Italian varietal wine, such as nebbiolo.

manfredi's comment
Having had the good fortune to be a guest of the Pizzini family, I can say that Fred grows some of the best nebbiolo in the country and Katrina is one of the finest cooks in the King Valley. This hearty dish, found in northern Italy as well as France, calls for a wine that is not overly fruity, with good tannin structure.

Left: Fred and Katrina Pizzini and Fred's parents Robert and Rose Pizzini

stanton & killeen wines

Rutherglen

Making fine fortified wine requires time and patience. Chris and Norman Killeen know this all too well, as their family have been producing such styles in Rutherglen since 1875. Some of the base-wine material incorporated into their illustrious reserve-blended styles dates back three generations.

The thick, multi-layered intensity of Stanton & Killeen's fortified wines must be sampled very slowly to be enjoyed to the full – complex levels of interest unfold with each mouthful. Their vintage port requires several decades' ageing if it's to be enjoyed in its prime.

The best way to enjoy these specialist wines is after dinner with coffee; or – at any time – with an array of dried fruits and nuts. This cheese and fruit platter is a great alternative to a dessert course and will make a superb accompaniment to a mature Stanton & Killeen vintage port.

pecorino & milawa blue cheese and vintage port
with fruit

Fresh Italian pecorino cheese
Milawa Blue cheese
Nashi
Dried apricots
Almonds
Plain biscuits

Avoid complicating the tastes. Choose 2 cheeses such as those suggested – one soft and one hard. Nashi (a cross between an apple and a pear) makes a succulent, crisp contrast in taste and texture to the cheeses. Dried apricots and plain almonds are an extra complement to the fresh fruit and cheese, and provide additional nutrition to the meal.

manfredi's comment
Port and blue cheese are a classic combination, though I think a well-aged, firm pecorino works as well. Make sure the cheeses are left out of the fridge for a good hour before serving. When served at room temperature, cheese exhibits all its wonderful flavours.

the green vineyards
Port Phillip

Sergio Carlei believes there are two types of wine – the first type he likens to breast implants: designed to attract attention at a distance, though on closer inspection revealing a lack of substance! The second type he sees as crafted specifically to complement food, and an integral part of the traditional European staple diet. These wines are restrained, yet reveal complexity and excitement with every sip. They flatter, rather than overpower, the meal. Sergio follows this philosophy when creating both of his labels, Carlei Estate and The Green Vineyards.

Sergio and his wife Mary (parents of seven children) have ample opportunity to test Sergio's theory at the (very large) family table. Friends and family alike enjoy Sergio's cooking, which is often traditional Italian – but in this meal, he demonstrates his flair for fusion cuisine. Of course, it pairs perfectly with his wine!

Sergio insists on the effectiveness of divining – it saves the costly operation of collecting and testing samples of water to use in the vineyards.

carlei thai-style mussels and carlei tre rossi
with ciabatta

2 tbsp sesame oil
1 onion, sliced
1 hot chilli, thinly sliced
1 tbsp chopped lemongrass
2 tspn chopped fresh ginger
1 tomato, diced
2 kaffir lime leaves
2 red capsicums, thinly sliced
1 kg fresh mussels
1 glass white wine
1 bunch fresh coriander, to garnish
8 thick slices toasted ciabatta

cook and serve
Heat sesame oil in heavy pan. Fry onion, chilli, lemongrass and ginger until transparent. Add tomato and lime leaves and cook for a few minutes. Add capsicum and cook for another few minutes. Add mussels and wine. Cover and cook, stirring occasionally, until mussel shells open. Discard those that do not open.

Serve mussel mixture in soup bowls and garnish with coriander. Provide two pieces of toasted ciabatta with each serving. Accompany with Carlei Estate Tre Rossi.

manfredi's comment
One of the most surprising food and wine matches for me was a Thai curry with a lightly chilled unwooded pinot noir. For a summer's day, try chilling Tre Rossi before tucking into these lovely mussels.

Above: Sergio Carlei with son Aaron

tasmania

apsley gorge vineyard
moorilla estate
rosevears estate

apsley gorge vineyard

Bicheno

Former abalone diver Brian Franklin is relieved that he and his colleague Greg Walch opted for grapes over sheep as the destiny of their Apsley Gorge property. Since its first vintage in 1995, Apsley Gorge has been commanding attention and winning awards for its full, luscious chardonnay and spicy, brooding pinot noir.

Apsley Gorge wines are a perfect match for the abundant fresh seafood at the winery doorstep – which happens to be the striking, untamed northeast shores of Tasmania.

steamed tasmanian blue mussels and chardonnay
with green salad and crusty bread

2 tbsp virgin olive oil
1 tsp fresh cracked pepper
1 clove of garlic, chopped
2 spring onions, finely chopped
1 kg Tasmanian blue mussels
1 cup fish stock
1 handful chopped parsley
1/2 bottle chardonnay

cook and serve
Heat oil, then add pepper, garlic and spring onion. Cook. Add mussels. Toss mixture and cover for a few minutes. (This extracts the flavour from the mussel shells.) Add stock, parsley and chardonnay. Cover and steam until shells open.

Serve in bowls with the cooking liquids and eat from the shell. Mop up juices with crusty bread, serve with green salad and enjoy with Tasmanian chardonnay.

manfredi's comment
Tasmanian mussels are my favourite, and this dish is a testament to simplicity as a primary virtue in cooking. As the mussels open they release their salty liquor, combining with the chardonnay to produce something special.

Below: Brian Franklin

moorilla estate

Berriedale

Enchanting garden settings and an open-air a'-la-carte restaurant give the feeling of being far, far away from it all, yet Moorilla Estate is only a 15-minute drive from Hobart.

Over the past few years, Moorilla Estate's manager, Tim Goddard, and winemaker, Alain Rousseau, have been busy cementing this long-established winery's reputation for excellence. Their passion and enthusiasm shine through in their wines, as well as in the restaurant.

Moorilla Estate has earned its reputation with classic cool-climate styles. The St Matthias label encompasses a selection of easy-drinking wines. Moorilla's Jason Winter Collection was created in memory of the estate's former winemaker, a victim of the Port Arthur massacre.

roast marinated quail and pinot noir
with porcini mushroom risotto cake and pinot noir jus

prepare the quail
Marinate butterflied quail with sesame oil, kecap manis, star anise, cinnamon quills, fresh ginger and lemongrass for at least 24 hours.

cook the risotto cakes and quail
Add 1 cup of chopped and soaked porcini mushrooms, 100 g butter and some grated parmesan cheese to a cooked risotto. Mix together well, pour into a tray and set in the refrigerator. When set, cut into squares and sear in a hot pan, then finish in the oven for 5 minutes at 180ºC. Sear quail in a hot pan, then roast until cooked. Remove the quail, add stock and pinot noir to pan and reduce to make a jus.

To serve, stack some steamed greens, the risotto cake and the quail on the jus. Serve the dish with slightly chilled pinot noir.

manfredi's comment
Quail is every bit as compatible with pinot noir as duck, though easier to prepare. Be certain to sear the quail skin until it is golden, to maximise those complex flavours of sweet soy, star anise, ginger and cinnamon that are so good to pinot noir.

Left: Tim Goddard and chef Paul Brown

rosevears estate

Rosevears

Dr Michael Beamish dreamed of a major tourism venture, to marry food, wine and magnificent views. Two decades ago the dream was realised at Notley Gorge Vineyard in western Tamar, northern Tasmania. Since 1999, wines from Notley Gorge have been sold under the Rosevears label. This cold-climate state is reputed for its aromatic, light-bodied wines. The unique gravel soils and ample sunshine of Rosevears allow for the production of a robust, award-winning cabernet sauvignon.

Michael – a haematologist – runs a full-time medical practice and spends weekends tending to the wine business. He and his wife Christina relish every opportunity to take time out from their hectic schedule to enjoy a quiet glass of red with a fine meal.

confit of duck and cabernet sauvignon
with marinated red cabbage

prepare and cook the duck
Grind together whole black peppercorns, star anise and cloves. Add lemon zest and orange zest. Place over 6 duck legs, cover and leave overnight. Cook in duck fat to cover, in a moderate oven (180°C), for approximately 2 hours.

cook the cabbage
Marinate half a thinly sliced red cabbage overnight in:
100 g redcurrant jelly
1 small red onion, finely chopped
1 diced granny smith apple
3 cloves
2 tsp cinnamon
125 mL orange juice
60 mL red wine vinegar
200 g brown sugar
125 mL cabernet sauvignon

Cook the marinated cabbage mixture, covered, on low heat for 1 hour prior to dinner, then cook uncovered for 20 minutes. Mound cabbage in the centre of the plate and arrange duck legs on top. Serve with a glass of good cabernet sauvignon.

manfredi's comment
The aromatic mix of spices in this duck confit adds to the complexity of the dish as well as providing a dynamic foil for the rich flesh of the duck. I especially love the "sweet and sour" cabbage as an accompaniment, sitting well across the riper Tamar cabernet.

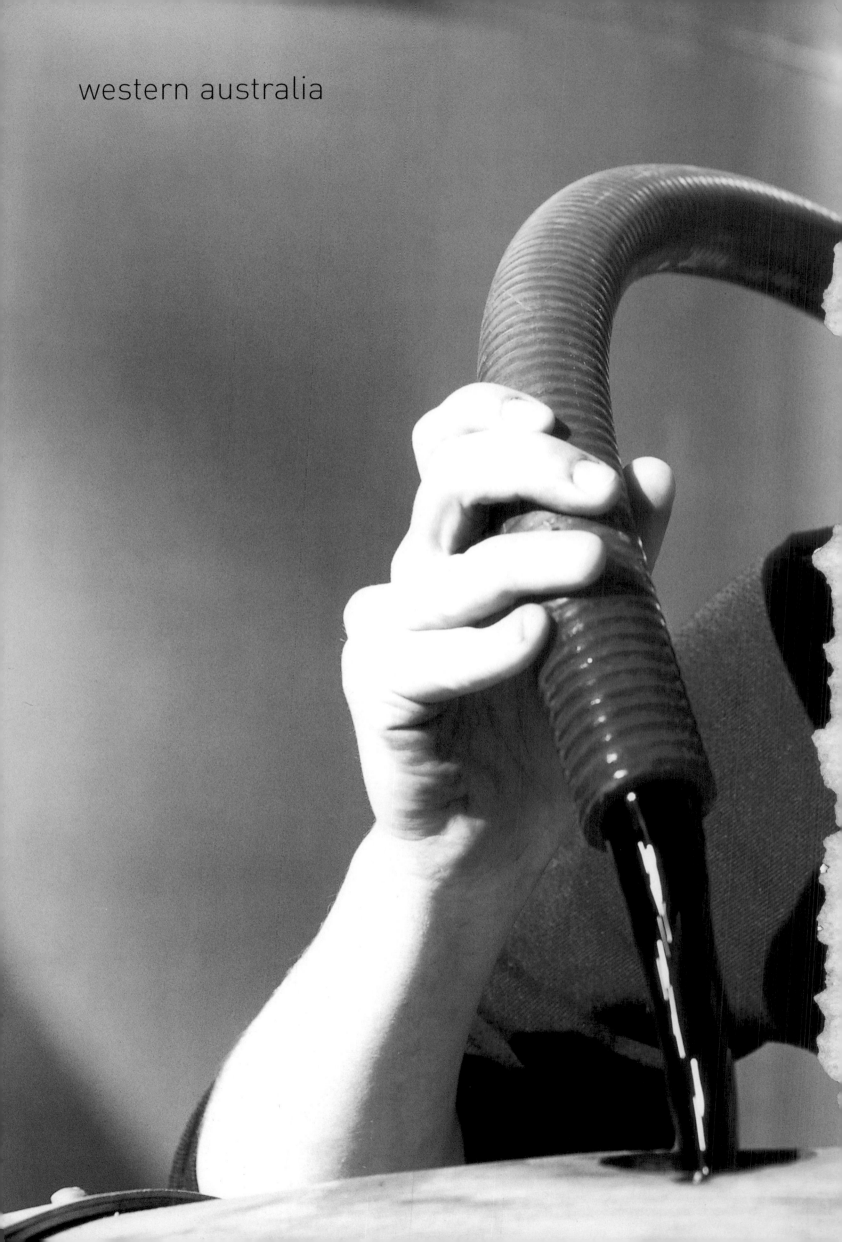

western australia

Though grapes are grown successfully from the Swan Valley in the north to Albany in the south, Western Australia's most productive group of regions is around Margaret River and Pemberton, and this area has a great abundance of saltwater and freshwater fare.

The southwest region of WA is a goldmine. Its fertile soils and tall trees have been and still are a great source of fruit, dairy, beef, sheep and timber products. More recently, though, quality produce such as asparagus, venison and, freshwater marron are earning renown, and let's not forget the plethora of sea life – abalone, crayfish, dhufish, tuna, sardines, blue swimmer crabs – supplied by the Indian and Southern Oceans.

Growing up around the Margaret River region, with its forests, wild, open coast and protected bays meant that if you couldn't find something to eat, there was something wrong! Recollections of being battered against rocks while clinging to bits of weed, just to get that elusive abalone stuck in the crevice, then scoffing it hot as it comes off the barbecue, lightly cooked in butter lemon and garlic... these taste memories will never fade.

The region has attracted settlers from all walks of life, but something which links them all is a passion for culinary experiences. Festivals celebrating the region's wealth of produce and the marriage of foods and wines highlight this. The following pages are full of WA winemakers proud of their harvest... read on!

sardines filled with pinenut paste, baked in red wine

4 fresh sardines
2 tbsp pinenuts
2 roasted garlic cloves, peeled
1 tbsp chopped Italian parsley
2 tsp lemon juice
2 tsp virgin olive oil
Salt and pepper, to taste
1 cup red wine and 1/2 cup olive oil, for poaching

Brush a deep baking dish with oil. Cut sardines along the belly from head to tail, remove entrails and backbone, then rinse under cold water and dry. Lay on baking dish. Toast the pinenuts until golden. Crush the pinenuts, garlic, parsley, lemon juice, oil, salt and pepper in a mortar and pestle or in a blender. Fill the sardines with the paste, pour wine and oil into baking dish and bake at 160ºC for 15 minutes.

Serve warm or cold, with red or white wine.

Ely Jarvis
Fonty's Pool, Pemberton, WA

Western Australia

cullen wines
flinders bay
fonty's pool
happs
joseph river estate
redgate wines
wignalls wines
woodlands wines
woody nook

cullen wines

Margaret River

Di Cullen and her late husband, Dr Kevin Cullen, pioneered grape-growing in Margaret River in 1971 – at a time when the region was most famous for its surf beaches and caves. Their multi-talented winemaker daughter Vanya continues the family tradition, producing wines of excellence in their estate winery.

Vanya divides her hectic schedule between winemaking, wine judging and assisting her mother in managing the business, which includes a busy cellar door and restaurant.

Right: Vanya Cullen

Manfredi's comment
The lean and slightly sweet nature of venison lends itself beautifully to a focused, tightly structured cabernet: the hallmark of the Cullen family. When making the sage and garlic paste, try using a mortar and pestle for a full, creamier texture. It will take longer, but you'll find the result is well worth it.

venison and cabernet/merlot
with sweet potato & sticky onion pie

for each person:
4 sage leaves
1 tbsp virgin olive oil
1 clove of garlic
200 g venison rump
1 cup Cullen cabernet/merlot
1 cup venison stock
1 red onion
1 sweet potato
2 tbsp melted butter
Salt and pepper, to taste
1 tbsp sugar
2 tbsp butter
Salt and black pepper, to taste

marinate the venison
Make a paste from sage, oil and garlic. Flatten
venison with mallet. Rub paste into meat and
infuse with the wine for 24 hours. Drain, add
marinade to venison stock and reduce to 1/2 cup.

make the sweet potato & sticky onion pie
Peel and finely slice onion and sweet potato. Mix
sweet potato with half the melted butter and seasonings.
Fry onion slowly with sugar and remaining melted butter
until caramelised. Pack some of the sweet potato into
a mould, add a thin layer of onion, then a layer of
sweet potato. Bake in a moderately low oven
(150ºC) until golden.

to finish
Dry venison on paper towels and sauté quickly in
1 tbsp butter. Whip remaining butter into sauce
and season. Serve venison with sauce, pie and
roasted chokos.

flinders bay

Margaret River

Flinders Bay is in the southwest corner of West Australia. The untamed seas of the area are home to numerous shipwrecks and Flinders Bay Winery has named its semillion/sauvignon blanc blend, Pericles, after the largest shipwreck in the bay.

Some of the fruit for the wines is sourced from 30-year-old vines on a vineyard in nearby Witchcliffe that belongs to Alastair Gillespie, a former grower and now a partner in Flinders Bay. Another recently planted site in Karridale is a sign that the business is rapidly moving forward.

Alastair makes the most of his coastal locale, enjoying the opportunity to create a seafood extravaganza with his mobile mini-kitchen.

abalone and semillon/ sauvignon blanc
with garlic, ginger and chilli

prepare for a great beach bbq!
Remove the abalone from the shell.
Clean, then soften by hitting the centre
muscle firmly a few times with a hammer.
Rinse. Roll in plain flour. Heat light
vegetable oil in a pan until hot, then
add garlic, ginger and hot dried chilli
(including seeds). Add abalone and cook
for 1 minute. Drain on paper towels.

Serve with salads and a cool glass
of Flinders Bay white.

manfredi's comment
This dish screams out summer,
swimming and the taste of salt
on your skin. Classic Margaret River
white is as refreshing as a sea breeze
and the perfect accompaniment to the
assertive flavours of garlic, ginger and
chilli. Abalone brings a luxurious
quality to a dish that when prepared
simply, as Alastair does, is a treat
on a balmy late afternoon.

fonty's pool

Manjimup

Fonty's Pool vineyards were established in 1996 amid the picturesque forests of Manjimup. The brand was created as a joint venture with Cape Mentelle.

Horticulture-trained winemaker Eloise (Ely) Jarvis asserts that making great wines begins with premium-quality fruit. For this reason, she spends a lot of time in the vineyard, consulting with viticulturist Kevin Goodwin. The Fonty's Pool shiraz displays pepper characters and the firm tannins of its cool-climate origins, with oak beautifully understated.

As well as being passionate about wine, Ely brims with enthusiasm when she speaks about her favourite pastime – cooking. She is inspired by recipes from famous chefs and loves adapting their creations to incorporate the diverse range of local produce.

marinated grilled lamb sandwiches and shiraz
with grilled vegetables

the meat
1 spring lamb leg, boned and butterflied.
Rub crushed garlic, rosemary and pepper
into the cut side of the meat. Pour on lemon
juice and olive oil. Turn. Cover. Marinate
overnight. Preheat grill to very high.
Seal all sides. Continue to cook on lower
heat until done. Cool and slice.

the vegetables
Grill your choice of vegetables, including skinned
capsicum, sliced eggplant and zucchini. Coat
cooked vegetables with a mixture of olive oil,
lemon juice and garlic. Combine with marjoram,
basil leaves and rocket.

the finished product
Take sliced lamb and the vegetables, plus fresh
bread, on your next picnic, and take the
Fonty's Pool shiraz with you!

manfredi's comment

This is the perfect picnic parcel. Grill lamb especially for these gorgeous "panini", or use slices of leftover roast leg of lamb or shoulder. The grilled vegetables can be prepared ahead of time and allowed to marinate in a little olive oil. Take some chutney or mustard, and make sure the bread is crusty and there's plenty of shiraz.

happs
Dunsborough

Happs is best known for luscious, bold merlot. The family-owned winery produces a range of innovative wines from its two vineyards, Three Hills in Karridale and Happs in Dunsborough – both in the Margaret River region. Established in 1978 by Erl and Roslyn Happ, the business is very much a generational concern, now involving their son Myles, daughter-in-law Jacquie and their four children.

The family attach great importance to the food they prepare – often with the eager assistance of one of the children, and utilising pottery created by Myles.

perfectly fabulous pizza and red or white
with fresh herbs and vegetables

first make a yeast dough with plain flour

...then make the sauce and pizza base
Cook garlic, onions and freshly torn basil with fresh tomatoes. Allow dough to rise. Divide into pieces and roll out on a floured surface. Gently pull and tuck the edges underneath. Place the dough on a hot, oiled platter and spread on the delicious tomato sauce. Follow with grated mozzarella.

...now let the imagination run loose
Throw caramelised leek, prosciutto and any sliced vegetable on top of the sauce. Add black pepper, sunflower and pepita seeds, grated cheeses and fresh herbs. Bake until done. Add sour cream, basil or rocket leaves... mmmm.

Left: Rosie-Jane and Jacquie Happ
Right: Myles Happ and the kids

Manfredi's comment
Kids and adults alike enjoy pizza, both its making and its eating. And when it comes to wine, pizza is very forgiving and accommodating. The biggest mistake you can make is to overload it with a mountain of topping. It should be mostly about the base with a smattering of tasty tomato sauce, then the prudent use of a little imagination – one or two flavours tend to work best. Most light- to medium-bodied white or red wines will be perfect with pizza.

joseph river estate

Geographe

A newcomer to the scene, Joseph River Wines had its first vintage in 2000. This is the premium label of Harvey River Bridge Estate, located in the southwest corner of Western Australia, some 200 kilometres north of Margaret River. Joseph River produces classic regional styles, a lively, crisp semillon its flagship wine.

As well as running the winery, Laurie and Kevin Sorgiovani together operate the family business, Harvey Fresh, which focuses on the production of fresh orange juice. Kevin's busy schedule usually keeps him away from the kitchen, but when he does manage a night at home, he likes nothing more than to test–drive a few culinary creations on the family.

spaghetti marinara and semillon
with rocket salad

1 onion, chopped
2 cloves of garlic, chopped
1 red capsicum, chopped
Olive oil
2 x 400 g cans diced tomatoes
Salt and pepper, to taste
Basil, fresh or dried, chopped
King snapper
Wild mussels
Squid rings
Tiger prawns
Sea scallops
500 g spaghetti
Parmesan cheese, to serve

cook and serve
Fry onion, garlic and capsicum together in the oil. Add tomatoes and cook for 15 minutes. Add salt, pepper, and basil to taste. Add seafood to sauce and cook for a further 10-15 minutes. Meanwhile, cook spaghetti, then drain. Toss through sauce and sprinkle with parmesan cheese. Serve with a rocket salad and Joseph River semillon.

manfredi's comment

Crisp West Australian semillon is fabulous with all seafood, especially shellfish. The sweet, full flavour of wild Australian mussels is the star feature of this classic spaghetti and seafood dish. Remember to use the freshest of the catch for the best results.

Left: Laurie and Kevin Sorgiovani

191

redgate wines

Margaret River

Redgate was one of the first boutique wineries to be established in this prestigious region. The winery has established a strong following, especially for cabernet sauvignon. Bill Ullinger and son Paul are at the helm, though grape and wine production is very much a team effort. Utmost care and attention in the vineyard provides top-quality ripe grapes for winemaker Andrew Forsell, allowing him to create Redgate's award-winning wines.

Specialty local produce features in the Ullingers' favourite dishes, such as this stuffed beef fillet created by Chef Tony Howell of nearby Cape Lodge to partner Redgate's cabernet/merlot blend.

harvey beef fillet and cabernet/merlot blend
with spinach & goat's cheese stuffing

prepare and cook
Trim top-quality beef fillet and slice down one side.
Line with English spinach and fill with goat's cheese.
Fold fillet to a neat shape and tie with string. Season
and pan-grill on all sides. Bake at 200ºC until cooked
to taste, 15-20 minutes for rare to medium-rare.

Cut into 4 pieces and serve on field-mushroom
risotto cakes, with a glass of Margaret River cabernet/merlot.

Above: Chef Tony Howell of Cape Lodge with Paul Ullinger
Right: Workers in the Redgate Wines vineyard

manfredi's comment
Margaret River produces some of the best goat's
cheese and cabernet wines in the world, so it's no
coincidence that the cheese's tangy creaminess
goes so well with those finely grained tannins.
Be sure to cook the beef medium-rare at most,
to retain flavour from all those meat juices.

193

wignalls wines

Albany

Bill Wignall was the pioneering veterinarian in the Albany district in 1964. After extensive research, he discovered that Albany's summer climate parallels that of Burgundy. This inspired him to plant pinot noir and chardonnay in 1982 and made him one of the first proponents of wine production in the area.

The Wignall family are proud of their holistic approach in the vineyard. No insecticides have been used since 1989 and every vine receives tender, loving care. In addition, grapes are handpicked and all wines are carefully crafted in their own winery. The results of this labour of love are reflected in the powerful flavours exhibited in Wignalls wines. To accompany them, a family favourite is this hearty game dish prepared by Bill's daughter-in-law, Claire.

char-grilled venison and pinot noir
with sweet potato, roasted red capsicums, pesto, and pinot noir jus

3 large red capsicums
Virgin olive oil
Pesto (to make, see below)
2 large sweet potatoes
1 whole nutmeg, grated
1/3 cup breadcrumbs
2 tbsp margarine
Salt and pepper, to taste
8 prosciutto slices
4 venison fillets
1 brown onion, finely chopped
20 mL balsamic vinegar
1/2 bottle Wignalls pinot noir
500 mL veal demiglace
Puff pastry triangles, to garnish

pesto: Mince 3 cloves of garlic. Mix with chopped fresh basil and 60 g grated parmesan cheese. Blend in 40 mL balsamic vinegar and 100 mL olive oil.

prepare and cook
Brush capsicums with oil. Bake for 20 minutes, or until outer skin bubbles. Cover with damp towel for 10 minutes. Skin and remove seeds. Slice and cover with pesto to marinate.

Boil and mash sweet potato, adding nutmeg, breadcrumbs, half the margarine, and seasonings.

Wrap prosciutto around venison fillets and secure with a skewer. Brush with oil. Grill evenly to your taste. Be careful not to overcook. Melt remaining margarine in the grill pan and cook onion until soft. Add vinegar, wine and demiglace, and reduce to 1 cup of jus.

Serve venison with sweet potato, capsicum, jus, puff pastry triangles, and a bottle of pinot noir.

manfredi's comment
Venison is very lean meat, especially
the fillet. In this preparation, the prosciutto
takes the place of fat to protect the meat
as it grills. Use a little of the pinot noir to
capture the gamey flavours in the
venison drippings.

195

woodlands wines

Margaret River

Heather and David Watson established the Woodlands vineyards in 1973. In doing so, they were among the grape-growing pioneers of the region. Now, their children Stuart, Andrea and Elizabeth are involved in the business.

The vineyard is surrounded by jarrah, marri and blackbutt gums and is less than 2 kilometres from the ocean. The climate, soils and terroir of Margaret River are often likened to those of Bordeaux in France. Not surprisingly, it is Bordeaux-style cabernet-based wines that are Woodlands' specialty.

prime beef rib and cabernet
with potatoes, carrots and peas

Prime beef rib
20 mL extra virgin olive oil
60 mL cabernet
Potatoes, peeled
Carrots, peeled and sliced
Pepper and salt, to taste
Fresh green peas and Jolly Frog
Restaurant Béarnaise Sauce,
to serve

prepare and serve
Marinate the beef rib in oil and cabernet for 24 hours. Pat dry on paper towels, then seal on a hotplate and roast with potatoes and carrots in a moderate oven (180ºC) until done to your taste. Rest meat in a warm place for 10 minutes. Season to taste.

Serve and carve at the table, with roasted vegetables, peas and béarnaise sauce on the side.

manfredi's comment
An entire day marinating in Margaret River cabernet and extra virgin olive oil will impart an extraordinary flavour to the already exceptional beef rib. Once it is seared in a pan it will caramelise quickly, ready for the oven. The less it's cooked, the more flavour it will retain; so leave it rare or, at most, medium-rare.

woody nook wines

Margaret River

The Gallaghers first created their nook, surrounded by trees, in 1978. Neil Gallagher, second-generation winemaker, upholds the viticultural and winemaking tradition of his parents. The vines are dry-farmed, providing the amazing depth and concentration of fruit characters that feature in all of the Woody Nook wines.

The irresistible winery name has led to the naming of the on-site Nookery Café and the fortified wine, Nooky's Delight, showing that despite the serious quality of the wines, the winemakers are not averse to a bit of fun.

During the winter months, between harvests, Neil and partner Debbie Brown enjoy roast dinners by the open fire. The vineyard view from their kitchen window reminds them of many vintages yet to come.

roasted leg of venison and cabernet sauvignon
with roasted vegetables and venison/cabernet jus

venison/cabernet jus (prepared the day before)
Venison bones
Celery, trimmed and chopped
2 carrots, peeled and chopped
1 brown onion, peeled and chopped
Olive oil
2 tbsp tomato paste
1/2 L cabernet
1/2 L vegetable stock

Brown venison bones in large pot. Cover with water and boil. Brown celery, carrot and onion with a little oil in a pan, then add tomato paste, stir in, and add to venison stock. Deglaze browning pan with cabernet and add vegetable stock, then add this mixture to pot. Simmer very gently for 12 hours to reduce. Strain the jus and continue to reduce until thickened.

roast the venison
3.5 kg venison
Viva Late Harvest olive oil
Rosemary, chopped
Salt and pepper
Sage leaves, chopped
Roasting vegetables, of choice
Garlic cloves, peeled
Fresh pears
Asparagus
Spring onions, trimmed

Wash and dry meat. Rub over with Viva olive oil. Rub half the rosemary and the salt, pepper and sage over the meat. Roast at 190ºC for 25 minutes. Reduce heat to 170ºC and cook for a further 3 hours. Add roasting vegetables and garlic, pears and the remaining rosemary to the roasting pan for the last hour of cooking. Tie the asparagus into a bunch, using the spring onions, and steam, just before carving the meat.

Serve venison with the roasted vegetables (including garlic) and pears, the steamed asparagus and spring onions, and the jus. Accompany with our cabernet!

manfredi's comment
Roasted venison with cabernet jus brings us back to the old adage recommending that you drink the same wine with the meal that you've used to cook it with. Once the jus has been strained, let it cool, then leave it in the refrigerator overnight so that the fat solidifies and can be removed easily before reheating.

Left: Debbie Brown, Karen Crawford and Neil Gallagher

contacts

Allandale Winery
Tel: (02) 4990 4526
Lovedale Road, Lovedale NSW 2320
www.allandalewinery.com.au

All Saints Estate
Tel: (02) 6033 1922
All Saints Road, Wahgunyah VIC 3687
www.allsaintswine.com.au

Andrew Harris Vineyards
Tel: (02) 6373 1213
Sydney Road, Mudgee NSW 2850
www.andrewharris.com.au

Apsley Gorge Vineyard
Tel: (03) 6375 1221
The Gulch, Bicheno TAS 7215

Balgownie Estate
Tel: (03) 5449 6222
Hermitage Road, Maiden Gully VIC 3551
www.balgownie.com

Ballandean Estate
Tel: (07) 4684 1226
Sundown Road, Ballandean QLD 4382

Balnaves of Coonawarra
Tel: (08) 8737 2946
Main Road, Coonawarra SA 5263
www.balnaves.com.au

Bethany Wines
Tel: (08) 8563 2086
Bethany Road, Bethany via Tanunda SA 5352
www.bethany.com.au

Bimbadgen Estate
Tel: (02) 4998 7585
Lot 21, McDonalds Road, Pokolbin NSW 2321
www.binbadgen.com.au

Blue Wren Winery
Tel: (02) 6372 6205
Cassilis Road, Mudgee NSW 2850
www.bluewrenwines.com.au

Briar Ridge Vineyard
Tel: (02) 4990 3670
Mt View Road, Mt. View NSW 2325
www.briarridge.com.au

Brindabella Hills Winery
Tel: (02) 6230 2583
156 Woodgrove Close, via Hall ACT 2618

Burton Premium Wines
Tel: (02) 9403 1012
PO Box 242, Killara NSW 2071
www.burtonpremiunwines.com

Cambewarra Estate
Tel: (02) 4446 0170
520 Illaroo Road, Cambewarra NSW 2540
www.cambewarra.com.au

Cape Jaffa Wines
Tel: (08) 8768 5053
Limestone Coast Road, Cape Jaffa
via Robe SA 5276
www.capejaffawines.com.au

Casa Freschi
Tel: (08) 8536 4569
30 Jackson Ave, Strathalbyn SA 5255
www.casafreschi.comau

Casella Wines
Tel: (02) 6968 1346
Farm 1471 Wakely Road, Yenda NSW 2681

Chain of Ponds
Tel: (08) 8389 1415
Main Adelaide Road, Gumeracha SA 5233
www.chainofpondswines.com.au

Chambers Rosewood Winery
Tel: (02) 6032 8641
Barkly Street, Rutherglen VIC 3685

Charles Sturt University Winery
Tel: (02) 6933 2435
Boorooma Street, Wagga Wagga NSW 2678
www.csu.edu.au/winery

Chrismont Wines
Tel: (03) 5729 8220
Upper King Valley Road, Cheshunt VIC 3678
www.chrismontwines.com.au

Clonakilla
Tel: (02) 6227 5877
Crisps Lane, Murrumbateman NSW 2582
www.clonakilla.com.au

Cowra Estate
Tel: (02) 6342 1136
Boorowa Road, Cowra NSW 2794

Cullen Wines
Tel: (08) 9755 5277
Caves Road, Cowaramup WA 6284
www.cullenwines.com.au

Dal Zotto Wines
Tel : (03) 5729 8321
Edi Road, Cheshunt VIC 3678

Delatite Winery
Tel: (03) 5775 2922
Cnr Stoneys & Pollards Roads,
Mansfield VIC 3722

Elmswood Estate
Tel: (03) 5964 3015
75 Monbulk Seville Road, Wandin East VIC 3139
www.elmswoodestate.com.au

Flinders Bay
Tel: (08) 9757 6281
Wilson Road, Karridale WA 6288

Fonthill Wines
Tel: 0419 343 547
California Road, McLaren Vale SA 5171

Fonty's Pool
Tel: (08) 9757 3266
PO Box 110, Margaret River WA 6285
www.capementelle.com.au

Frog Rock
Tel: (02) 6372 2408
Lawson Farm, Edgell Lane,
Mudgee NSW 2850
www.tallara.com.au

Gapsted Wines
Tel: (02) 5751 1992
Great Alpine Road, Gapsted VIC 3737
www.gapstedwines.com.au

Gartelmann Hunter Estate
Tel: (02) 4930 7113
Lovedale Road, Lovedale NSW 2321
www.gartelmann.com.au

Goulburn Valley Estate Wines
Tel: (03) 5829 0278
340 Trotter Road, Mooroopna Nth VIC 3629

Hamiltons Bluff
Tel: (02) 6344 2079
Cnr Ryegates Lane & Longs Corner Rd,
Canowindra NSW 2804
www.worldwidewine.com.au

Happs
Tel: (08) 9755 3300
Commonage Road, Dunsdorough WA 6281
www.happs.com.au

Hollick Wines
Tel: (08) 8737 2318
Cnr Ravenswood Lane & Riddoch Highway,
Coonawarra SA 5263
www.hollick.com

Inigo
Lot 2 New England Highway
Glen Aplin QLD 4381

Joseph River Estate
Tel: (08) 9729 2199
Third Street, Harvey WA 6220

Knight Granite Hills Wines
Tel: (03) 5423 7264
1481 Burke & Wills Track, Baynton,
Kyneton VIC 3444

Kulkunbulla
Tel: (02) 4998 7358
Cnr Broke & Hermitage Rd,
Pokolbin NSW 2320
www.kulkunbulla.com.au

Lake Breeze Wines
Tel: (08) 8537 3017
Step Road, Langhorne Creek SA 5255
www.lakebreeze.com.au

Langmeil Winery
Tel: (08) 8563 2595
Cnr Langmeil and Para Rds,
Tanunda SA 5352
www.langmeilwinery.com.au

Leconfield Coonawarra
Tel: (08) 8556 2288
Riddock Highway, Coonawarra SA 5363
www.leconfield.com.au

Logan
Tel: (02) 9958 6844
160 Sailors Bay Road, Northbridge NSW 2063
www.loganwines.com.au

Macquariedale Estate
Tel: (02) 6574 7012
170 Sweetwater Road, Rothbury NSW 2335
www.macquariedale.com.au

Madew Wines
Tel: (02) 4848 0026
Westering Vineyard, The Vineyards,
Federal Highway, Lake George
Via Collector NSW 2581
www.madewwines.com.au

Massoni Homes
Tel: (03) 5989 2962
1058 Mornington Flinders Road,
Red Hill VIC 3937
www.massoniwines.com

Millfield
Tel: (02) 4998 1571
Lot 341 Mount View Road,
Millfield NSW 2325
www.millfieldwines.com

Moorilla Estate
Tel: (03) 6277 9900
655 Main Road, Berriedale TAS 7011
www.moorilla.com.au

Mount Avoca Vineyard
Tel: (03) 5465 3282
Moates Lane, Avoca VIC 3467
www.mountavoca.com

Padthaway Estate
Tel: (03) 98134355
Riddoch Highway, Padthaway SA 5271
www.padthawayestate.com.au

Paringa Estate
Tel: (03) 5989 2669
44 Paringa Road, Red Hill South VIC 3937
www.paringaestate.com.au

Peacock Hill Vineyard
Tel: (02) 4998 7661
Palmers Lane, Pokolbin NSW 2320.

Peter Rumball Wines
Tel: (08) 8332 2761
55 Charles Street, Norwood SA 5067
www.rumball.com.au

Pizzini Wines
Tel: (03) 5729 8278
RMB 9591 King Valley Rd, Whitfield VIC 3678
www.pizzini.com.au

Ralph Fowler Wines
Tel: (08) 8768 5000
Lot 101 Limestone Coast Road,
Kingston SA 5275

Ravenswood Lane
Tel: (08) 8388 1250
Ravenswood Lane, Hahndorf SA 5245
www.ravenswoodlane.com.au

RBJ Vintners
Tel: (08) 8524 6821
PO Box 34, Tanunda SA 5352

Redgate Wines
Tel: (08) 9757 6488
Boodjidup Road, Margaret River WA 6285
www.redgatewines.com.au

Rockford Wines
Tel: (08) 8563 2720
Krondorf Road, Tanunda SA 5352

Rosevears Estate
Tel: (03) 6330 1800
1A Waldhorn Drive, Rosevears TAS 7277
www.rosevearsestate.com

Rothvale Vineyard and Winery
Tel: (02) 4998 7290
Deasys Road, Pokolbin NSW 2321
www.users.bigpond.com/rothvalehunterhabit

Rusden Wines
Tel: (08) 8563 2976
Magnolia Road, Tanunda SA 5352

Ryan Family Wines
Tel: (02) 6579 1065
Broke Estate, Wollombi Road, Broke NSW 2330
www.ryanwines.com.au

Saddler's Creek Wines
Tel: (02) 4991 1770
Cnr Marrowbone and Oakey Creek Roads,
Pokolbin NSW 2320
www. saddlerscreekwines.com.au

Schild Estate Wines
Tel: (08) 8524 5560
Cnr Barossa Valley Highway
& Lyndoch Valley Road, Lyndoch SA 5351
www.schildestate.com.au

Simon Gilbert Wines
Tel: (02) 6373 1245
Appletree Flat via Mudgee NSW 2850

Simon Hackett Wines
Tel: (08) 8323 7712
Budgens Road, McLaren Vale SA 5171

Sirromet Wines
Tel: (07) 3206 2999
850-938 Mount Cotton Road,
Mount Cotton QLD 4165
www.mountcottonestate.com

Stanton & Killeen Wines
Tel: (02) 6032 9457
Jacks Road, Murray Valley Highway,
Rutherglen VIC 3685

Tapestry Wines
Tel: (08) 8323 9196
Olivers Road, McLaren Vale SA 5171
www.merrivale.com.au

Tempus Two Wines
Tel: (02) 4998 7521
Hermitage Road, Pokolbin NSW 2039
www.tempustwo.com.au

The Green Vineyards
Tel: (03) 5944 4599
Lot 2 Albers Road, Upper Beaconsfield VIC 3808
www.thegreenvineyards.com.au

The Silos Estate
Tel: (02) 4448 6082
640 Princes Highway,
Jaspers Brush NSW 2540
www.thesilos.com

Turkey Flat Vineyards
Tel: (08) 8563 2851
Bethany Road, Tanunda SA 5352
www.turkeyflat.com.au

Whisson Lake
Tel: (08) 8390 1303
Gully Road, Carey Gully SA 5142
www.whissonlake.com

Wignalls Wines
Tel: (08) 9841 2848
Chester Pass Road, (Highway 1),
King River, Albany WA 6330
www.wignallswines.com.au

Woodlands Wines
Tel: (08) 9755 6226
Lot 1, Caves Road, Willyabrup WA 6280

Woody Nook Wines
Tel: (08) 9755 7547
RSM 395, Metricup Road, Metricup WA 6280
www.woodynook.com.au